NEW DIRECTIONS FOR TEACHING AND LEARNING

Marilla D. Svinicki, *University of Texas, Austin*
EDITOR-IN-CHIEF

R. Eugene Rice, *American Association for Higher Education*
CONSULTING EDITOR

Scholarship Revisited: Perspectives on the Scholarship of Teaching

Carolin Kreber
University of Alberta

EDITOR

Number 86, Summer 2001

JOSSEY-BASS
San Francisco

SCHOLARSHIP REVISITED: PERSPECTIVES ON THE SCHOLARSHIP OF TEACHING
Carolin Kreber (ed.)
New Directions for Teaching and Learning, no. 86
Marilla D. Svinicki, Editor-in-Chief
R. Eugene Rice, Consulting Editor

Microfilm copies of issues and articles are available in 16mm and 35mm, as well as microfiche in 105mm, through University Microfilms Inc., 300 North Zeeb Road, Ann Arbor, Michigan 48106-1346.

ISSN 0271-0633   ISBN 0-7879-5447-0

NEW DIRECTIONS FOR TEACHING AND LEARNING is part of The Jossey-Bass Higher and Adult Education Series and is published quarterly by Jossey-Bass Inc., 350 Sansome Street, San Francisco, California 94104-1342. Periodicals postage paid at San Francisco, California, and at additional mailing offices. Postmaster: Send address changes to New Directions for Teaching and Learning, Jossey-Bass Inc., 350 Sansome Street, San Francisco, California 94104-1342.

New Directions for Teaching and Learning is indexed in College Student Personnel Abstracts, Contents Pages in Education, and Current Index to Journals in Education (ERIC).

SUBSCRIPTIONS cost $59.00 for individuals and $114.00 for institutions, agencies, and libraries. Prices subject to change.

EDITORIAL CORRESPONDENCE should be sent to the editor-in-chief, Marilla D. Svinicki, The Center for Teaching Effectiveness, University of Texas at Austin, Main Building 2200, Austin, TX 78712-1111.

Cover photograph by Richard Blair/Color & Light © 1990.

www.josseybass.com

Printed in the United States of America on acid-free recycled paper containing 100 percent recovered waste paper, of which at least 20 percent is postconsumer waste.

CONTENTS

1

The editor of this volume presents the results of the Delphi study, the framework for the chapters selected for this volume, and the positions taken in these chapters.

Conceptualizing the Scholarship of Teaching and Identifying Unresolved Issues: The Framework for This Volume

Carolin Kreber

The literature on the scholarship of teaching has been steadily expanding since Boyer (1990) introduced the concept a decade ago (for example, Edgerton, Hutchings, and Quinlan, 1991; Glassick, Huber, and Maeroff, 1997; Menges, Weimer, and Associates, 1995; Paulsen and Feldman, 1995; Richlin, 1993; Shulman, 1998). When we consider all the important and thoughtful work that is being done, is there any more to be gained from yet another book on the topic?

This volume is motivated by two considerations. First, despite the growing literature in the area, there is still confusion regarding the meaning of "scholarship of teaching," with different people espousing different definitions. Second, I think that unless the members of the academy come to agree on a definition, it will be very difficult to promote, demonstrate, assess, and institutionalize the concept in our universities.

This volume is the outcome of a study I conducted from 1998 to 1999 with an international panel of experts in the scholarship of teaching. The study pursued three goals: (1) to achieve consensus among a group of experts on what they perceive are important components of the scholarship of teaching, (2) to achieve consensus on what they perceive are unresolved issues surrounding the notion, and (3) to offer suggestions on how to address these problems in the form of a special *New Directions for Teaching and Learning* volume. Clearly, identifying experts in an area generally recognized as being ill-defined and elusive is problematic. Perhaps, ironically, one could challenge the criteria used in this study to select experts from at least two angles, depending on how one views the scholarship of teaching. One could argue that the criteria were not sufficiently inclusive, not descriptive enough of the various aspects of the scholarship of teaching that can be observed. Conversely, one could argue that the criteria were not sufficiently exclusive, not of sufficient discriminatory power to differentiate competence from expertise.

All eleven participants in the study are academics who enjoy an excellent reputation for their scholarly work on postsecondary teaching and learning and faculty evaluation; most of them have published explicitly on the scholarship of teaching. The panel was international in scope, with two participants from Canada, one from Australia, and eight from the United States. They were (in alphabetical order) Barbara Cambridge, director of the teaching initiatives for the American Association for Higher Education; John A. Centra, research professor and professor emeritus at Syracuse University, Higher Education Program; Patricia A. Cranton, honorary research scholar at the University of New Brunswick; Robert M. Diamond, president of the National Academy for Academic Leadership; Michael B. Paulsen, professor of higher education at the University of New Orleans; Paul Ramsden, pro-vice-chancellor of teaching and learning at the University of Sydney; Eugene Rice, scholar-in-residence and director of the Forum on Faculty Roles and Rewards at the American Association for Higher Education; Laurie Richlin, president of the International Alliance of Teacher Scholars; Lee S. Shulman, president of the Carnegie Foundation for the Advancement of Teaching; Ronald Smith, director of the Centre for the Enhancement of Learning and Teaching, City University of Hong Kong; and Michael Theall, director of the Center for Teaching and Learning at the University of Illinois at Springfield.

The Delphi Study

The study followed the Delphi survey method (Clayton, 1997; Fish and Busby, 1996; Linstone and Turoff, 1975) in that I collected data from each panelist separately, then compiled it, and subsequently shared responses with the entire panel without identifying individual respondents. However, all participants knew who else was on the panel. The study was conducted in three phases. The means for data collection was a questionnaire that was adapted with each phase.

Regarding panel size, Clayton (1997) suggests that there are no definite criteria; however, he recommends a panel of fifteen to thirty individuals if all the experts come from the same discipline and a smaller panel of five to ten individuals if each of the panelists has expertise on a particular topic but comes from a different discipline. A panel size of eleven for my study seemed appropriate, considering that participants did share higher education as a "discipline" from which to construe or frame the scholarship of teaching; this field itself, however, is interdisciplinary and therefore open to different areas of expertise.

Phase One. In October 1998, each participant was asked to respond in writing to two open-ended questions: (1) What do you consider to be the key features or components of the scholarship of teaching? (2) Which, if any, are the issues surrounding the scholarship of teaching that you consider to be unresolved to date? The deadline for turning in responses for this first phase was January 15, 1999.

I analyzed comments on each question in terms of individual statements made by the eleven respondents, who gave multiple responses to each question. The first question produced a total of forty-eight distinct statements, and the second a total of fifty-one discrete statements after identical comments had been summarized. With respect to the second question, six respondents mentioned the assessment of the scholarship of teaching as a problem, four raised concern regarding the lack of a clear definition of the scholarship of teaching, and three indicated that it is problematic that we do not know who should set the standards for review and evaluation. With nineteen of these fifty-one statements relating to the second question, participants did not only raise a problem or issue, as they did with the remaining thirty-two statements, but went beyond that initial assignment and actually took a stance on the issue itself (for example, offering an opinion on what should happen). Because this additional information was both interesting and useful, it was incorporated into the next phase of the survey.

Phase Two. On the basis of panelists' responses in Phase One of the survey, I developed a questionnaire that listed each distinct statement as a separate item. Phase Two's questionnaire consisted of three parts: Part I listed the forty-eight features or components of the scholarship of teaching that panelists had identified in response to question one, Part II listed the thirty-two unresolved issues identified in response to question two, and Part III listed those nineteen issues on which panelists had taken a stance. I added six additional items to Part III that originally had been raised in response to question two. For example, the statement "The lack of broadly acceptable definitions for the *scholarship of teaching, scholarly teaching, excellence in teaching, expert teacher* . . . is an unresolved issue" led me to produce the deliberately provocative item "An expert teacher is the same as a scholar of teaching." The questionnaire used in Phase Two of the Delphi study listed a total of 105 items (see Exhibit 1.1 on pp. 6–15).

In early February, I mailed this second questionnaire to each panelist with the instruction to rate each item on a seven-point Likert scale (1, "Strongly disagree," to 7, "Strongly agree") to indicate the extent to which he or she agreed with the statement. At this point, I also asked panelists to rank the five most important components of the scholarship of teaching as well as the five most important unresolved issues. All eleven questionnaires were returned by March 30, 1999. I analyzed ratings in terms of measures of central tendency and dispersion for each item. If the goal is to achieve consensus, the *median* (MDN), the point above and below which 50 percent of the responses fall, and *interquartile range* (IQR), containing the middle 50 percent of the responses, are more meaningful measures to be used than the mean and standard deviation, because extreme values on either end are ignored. The IQR's size indicates how widely the responses differed from one another: the greater the IQR, the more widespread the responses are and the less consensus there is among panelists. As there was not much agreement in terms of the items panelists selected as the five most important components of the scholarship of teaching (Part I) and the five most important unresolved issues (Part II), and in how they ranked them, the ranking data did not add much useful information and are not reported here.

Phase Three. In the third phase, individuals were invited to reconsider their initial response to each item in light of the group's rating. To this end, I adapted the questionnaire so as to report both the group's response and the individual panelists' initial responses to each item to compare. Only a few changes were made. A total of ten questionnaires were returned by April 30, 1999.

The results of Parts I and II of the third and final Delphi phase are reported in Exhibit 1.1. To stay with the terminology used when the study was conducted and to correspond to the terminology used by other contributors to this volume, results are reported in terms of agreement and consensus. Because these two terms are usually used synonymously, some clarification of how we apply these terms might be helpful. In this volume, readers are asked to think of *agreement* in terms of panelists' endorsement of or agreement with the item (reported in terms of the MDN). Readers are asked to think of *consensus* in terms of the measure of dispersion in the data, that is, the extent to which panelists agreed with each other (reported in terms of the IQR).

Results

The detailed findings of this study were first presented at the annual meeting of the Canadian Society for the Study of Higher Education (Kreber, 1999), and an overview was provided at the annual meeting of the American Educational Research Association (Kreber and Associates, 2000). Results are also reported in a research article (Kreber, forthcoming). This chapter concentrates on those findings that are most relevant to the chapters that follow. Exhibit 1.2 (see pp. 15–16) lists those items relating to Part I of the questionnaire that are most significant. As can be seen, panelists showed high agreement (MDN = 6.0–7.0) and strong consensus (IQR = 0–1.5) on eighteen features or components of the scholarship of teaching (listed under Category 1). As levels of agreement and consensus within this first category vary slightly, they are reported in three subcategories. Lower agreement (MDN = 5.0–5.5) but equally strong consensus (IQR = 0.5–1.5) was found on three additional items (listed under Category 2). Note that on a scale of 1 to 7 ("Strongly disagree" to "Strongly agree"), the notion of low agreement (MDN = 5.0) is not to be confused with disagreement, which would be represented by an MDN rating of 1, 2, or 3.

Exhibit 1.3 (see pp. 16–17) lists the most interesting items relating to Part II of the questionnaire. Panelists agreed, on the whole, yet to varying degrees (MDN = 4.5–7.0; IQR = 0.5–2.75) on twenty-one unresolved issues. These are reported in terms of four categories representing declining levels of agreement and consensus. Note that those items with which panelists did not agree (MDN < 4.5) do not appear in the exhibit.

The purpose of this volume is twofold: to present the scholarship of teaching in a way that is consistent with the results reported in Exhibit 1.2 and to explore most of the identified unresolved issues listed in Exhibit 1.3 in greater depth. Each contributor either volunteered for or was presented with some specific issues (we discuss sixteen of the twenty-one issues identified as unresolved in this volume) and was given the challenging task to propose creative and innovative ways to address these. Further, each contributor was encouraged to show, whenever feasible, how the underlying construct or definition of the scholarship of teaching espoused in his or her chapter relates to the results reported in Exhibit 1.2.

Overview of Subsequent Chapters

In the next chapter, Michael Paulsen provides a thought-provoking discussion of the relationship between research and the scholarship of teaching. Specifically, he discusses the linkages between the scholarship of teaching and the literature on teacher research and action research (item 5, Part II), between formal educational research and contextual classroom research (item 6), and between the scholarship of discovery on teaching and learning in higher education and the scholarship of teaching (item 11) (see Exhibit 1.3). In Chapter Three, Michael Theall and John Centra illustrate in creative ways how the scholarship of teaching could be assessed, recognized, and rewarded (item 2). Their discussion directly addresses the question of who should determine the standards and criteria by which to review and critique the scholarship of teaching (item 3) and whether all studies in the scholarship of teaching should be required to include authentic indicators of student learning and development (item 8). Maryellen Weimer, in Chapter Four, provides an in-depth exploration of the approaches to identify, codify, report, and communicate the wisdom of practice (item 32). In Chapter Five, Laurie Richlin offers her insights regarding the lack of broadly acceptable definitions for the scholarship of teaching and scholarly teaching (item 1). She discusses whether and to what extent the scholarship of teaching is something that all academics can practice (item 12) and whether publication of experience or findings in peer-reviewed media is a necessary characteristic of the scholarship of teaching (item 4). How teachers can acquire the knowledge and skills to become more scholarly in teaching (item 31) is illustrated by means of many practical examples. In Chapter

Six, Ronald Smith also differentiates the scholarship of teaching from other related constructs (item 1), but this time with particular emphasis on the links between expertise in teaching and expertise in the scholarship of teaching (items 27 and 30). In Chapter Seven, I share some suggestions with regard to how the scholarship of teaching could be built into graduate and faculty development programs (items 21 and 28). In Chapter Eight, Cynthia Weston and Lynn McAlpine demonstrate how the scholarship of teaching can be promoted at a research-intensive university. Specifically, they address the question of whether a scholar of teaching studies teaching as a discipline in itself or whether teaching is studied through another discipline (item 13). Furthermore, they make suggestions for how the isolation of the scholarship of teaching from the primary work of the disciplines and of departments might be overcome (item 15). Finally, in Chapter Nine, my intent is to provide some observations and reflections on what has been presented in this volume and to speculate further on how future work could be built on these findings.

Exhibit 1.1. The Scholarship of Teaching Questionnaire: Delphi Phase III

Please reconsider your responses to each item in light of the new information presented, and change your rating if you wish. The new information summarizes the responses of all other panelists to each item rated in Delphi Phase Two. The information is reported in terms of the median (MDN) and the interquartile range (IQR). The median is the point above and below which 50 percent of the responses fell. The interquartile range contains the middle 50 percent of the responses. Its size gives an indication of how widely the responses differed from one another; i.e., the greater the interquartile range, the more widespread the responses were, and the less consensus there is among panelists. Your previous answers to each item on the Delphi Questionnaire, Phase Two, are given for you to compare. Unless otherwise indicated, the analyses are based on eleven responses.

Part I

Question: What do you consider to be the key features or components of the scholarship of teaching?

Directions: For each of the items listed below, please indicate the extent to which you agree or disagree by assigning a rating between 1 and 7.

Scale

Strongly disagree   1   2   3   4   5   6   7   Strongly agree

1. A key feature in the scholarship of teaching is having an understanding of how people learn, knowing what practices are most effective, and having knowledge about what we have learned about teaching.

MDN   6.0   IQR 1.0   Your previous rating _____   Your new response _____

2. Those who practice the scholarship of teaching carefully design ways to examine, interpret, and share learning about teaching. Thereby they contribute to the scholarly community of their discipline.

MDN   7.0   IQR 1.0   Your previous rating _____   Your new response _____

3. The scholarship of teaching involves knowing where and why students have difficulty.

MDN   5.0   IQR 2.0   Your previous rating _____   Your new response _____

4. The key features of the scholarship of teaching are content knowledge in the deepest sense and knowledge of pedagogy in the broadest sense, resulting in pedagogical content knowledge.

MDN   6.0   IQR 3.0   Your previous rating _____ Your new response _____

5. Those activities that contribute to the advancement of pedagogical content knowledge constitute acts of scholarship.

MDN   6.0   IQR 2.0   Your previous rating _____ Your new response _____

6. The conduct of research on teaching and learning (less formal and formal) contributes to the advancement of pedagogical content knowledge and presents forms of the scholarship of discovery that overlap with, and are part of, the scholarship of teaching.

MDN   6.0   IQR 2.0   Your previous rating _____ Your new response _____

7. Graduate training and new faculty preparation that promote understanding of the complex interplay between research in the content of the discipline, traditional educational research on teaching and learning, and the processes of designing effective learning environments, in combination, constitute an act of scholarship.

MDN   5.0   IQR 2.0   Your previous rating _____ Your new response _____

8. People practicing the scholarship of teaching succeed in winning grants for their work.

MDN   3.0   IQR 2.0   Your previous rating _____ Your new response _____

9. The scholarship of teaching involves constant reflection of the process and outcomes of teaching and learning and acknowledges the contextual nature of teaching.

MDN   6.0   IQR 2.0   Your previous rating _____ Your new response _____

10. Scholarly teaching and the scholarship of teaching are both important to the life of the academy, but they are not the same.

MDN   6.0   IQR 3.0   Your previous rating _____ Your new response _____

11. Scholarly teaching is intended to have an impact on the activity of teaching. The scholarship of teaching is intended to result in a formal peer-reviewed communication in appropriate media or venues.

MDN   4.0   IQR 4.0   Your previous rating _____ Your new response _____

12. People practicing the scholarship of teaching can coherently link their discipline or professional knowledge with their knowledge of teaching.

MDN   6.0   IQR 2.0   Your previous rating _____ Your new response _____

13. People practicing the scholarship of teaching focus on change; they develop their practice through a cycle of action, reflection, and improvement.

MDN   6.0   IQR 2.0   Your previous rating _____ Your new response _____

14. Scholarship is the systematized knowledge of the expert. As such, it exhibits accuracy, validity, critical thought, and thoroughness. The scholarship of teaching is the knowledge of the expert teacher.

MDN   5.0   IQR 3.0   Your previous rating _____ Your new response _____

15. People practicing the scholarship of teaching need to have assessment, evaluation, and research skills. They need to be able to conduct classroom research and document the process of teaching and learning and student progress.

MDN   6.0   IQR 2.0   Your previous rating _____ Your new response _____

16. Excellent teachers need not be scholars of teaching.

MDN   6.0   IQR 5.0   Your previous rating _____ Your new response _____

17. People practicing the scholarship of teaching publish their findings.

MDN 5.0   IQR 2.0   Your previous rating _____ **Your new response** _____

18. The scholarship of teaching is an activity that, in the context of promoting student learning, meets each of the following criteria:

- Requires high levels of discipline-related expertise

- Breaks new ground and is innovative

- Can be replicated and elaborated

- Can be documented

- Can be peer reviewed

- Has significance or impact

MDN 6.0   IQR 2.0   Your previous rating _____ **Your new response** _____

19. Substantial portions of what constitutes the scholarship of teaching are discipline-specific. Hence, there is a strong need for research on teaching and learning in the disciplines.

MDN 6.0   IQR 2.0   Your previous rating _____ **Your new response** _____

20. People practicing the scholarship of teaching make a deliberate effort to share their experience with others (they act as mentors, communicators, faculty developers, and so on).

MDN 6.0   IQR 2.0   Your previous rating _____ **Your new response** _____

21. Faculty who practice the scholarship of teaching are curious about the ways in which students learn and the effects of certain practices on that learning.

MDN 7.0   IQR 1.0   Your previous rating _____ **Your new response** _____

22. Instructional development and evaluation that promote faculty awareness of how principles of effective instruction, based on traditional research, can be used to transform content knowledge into pedagogical content knowledge constitute acts of scholarship.

MDN 5.0   IQR 3.0   Your previous rating _____ **Your new response** _____

23. For people who practice the scholarship of teaching, teaching is driven by an inquiry ethic.

MDN 6.0   IQR 1.0   Your previous rating _____ **Your new response** _____

24. People practicing the scholarship of teaching need to be able to motivate.

MDN 4.0   IQR 4.0   Your previous rating _____ **Your new response** _____

25. Scholars of teaching are characterized by all of the following features (each should be present):

- They have comprehensive knowledge of the research and literature on teaching and learning.
- They conduct research and writing on teaching and learning and have experience in teaching.
- They have comprehensive knowledge of the practice of teaching, based on their teaching.
- They engage in critical reflection on teaching.
- They engage in innovations in teaching.
- They can demonstrate the validity of the knowledge of teaching they hold, through assessment by others, including students, peers, and administrators.

MDN 6.0   IQR 3.0   Your previous rating _____ **Your new response** _____

26. People who practice the scholarship of teaching do not make a sharp distinction between research and findings about student learning and classroom practice; they consider teaching a project in progress.

MDN   5.0   IQR 3.0   Your previous rating _____   Your new response _____

27. The scholarship of teaching involves making effective linkages and sequences that help learners progress toward more complex and sophisticated understanding.

MDN   5.0   IQR 3.0   Your previous rating _____   Your new response _____

28. While scholarly teaching is based on reflective observation and discussion of results, and evaluation of the teaching process by peers, the scholarship of teaching is based on extensive documentation of methods and results, integration of results into literature, comprehensive communication to peers, a submission for peer review, and, if accepted, publication and presentation.

MDN   5.0   IQR 4.0   Your previous rating _____   Your new response _____

29. The scholarship of teaching requires that teachers constantly reinterpret, integrate, and apply knowledge in their disciplines. This embellishes their teaching.

MDN   5.5   IQR 3.0   Your previous rating _____   Your new response _____

30. People practicing the scholarship of teaching are able to choose (via extended reflection and on-the-spot decision making) the best and most successful strategies.

MDN   4.0   IQR 4.0   Your previous rating _____   Your new response _____

31. People practicing the scholarship of teaching see the four areas (the scholarship of teaching, discovery, integration, and application) as overlapping entities.

MDN   6.0   IQR 3.0   Your previous rating _____   Your new response _____

32. The scholarship of teaching has characteristics that make it different from other forms of scholarship, but it also has characteristics that encompass the dimensions of the scholarship of discovery, integration, and application.

MDN   7.0   IQR 0.25 Your previous rating _____   Your new response _____

33. The scholarship of teaching needs to be integrated into and built upon other forms of scholarly work.

MDN   6.0   IQR 2.25 Your previous rating _____   Your new response _____

34. Enacting the wisdom of practice, that is, reflecting on the experience of teaching, and applying general principles of effective teaching and learning that enhance opportunities for learners to make connections between prior knowledge and new content constitute acts of scholarship.

MDN   5.0   IQR 3.0   Your previous rating _____   Your new response _____

35. Scholarly teachers teach for understanding and thinking skills; content knowledge is not enough.

MDN   6.0   IQR 2.25 Your previous rating _____   Your new response _____

36. Scholarly teachers are always learning both about knowledge in their field and how to make connections with students.

MDN   6.0   IQR 2.00 Your previous rating _____   Your new response _____

37. People who practice the scholarship of teaching show leadership in teaching.

MDN   4.0   IQR 1.75 Your previous rating _____   Your new response _____

38. A key feature in the scholarship of teaching is the hard intellectual work that goes into preparing effective learning experiences for students.

MDN   5.0   IQR 1.25 Your previous rating _____   Your new response _____

39. Individuals practicing the scholarship of teaching investigate the relationship between teaching and learning.

MDN   6.5   IQR 1.25   Your previous rating _____   **Your new response** _____

40. People who practice the scholarship of teaching generate new ideas about teaching.

MDN   6.0   IQR 2.0   Your previous rating _____   **Your new response** _____

41. Engaging in classroom research is important but is not sufficient for the scholarship of teaching.

MDN   6.0   IQR 1.25   Your previous rating _____   **Your new response** _____

42. The scholarship of teaching includes research and publication, but this is not the primary component of a scholarship of teaching.

MDN   6.0   IQR 2.25   Your previous rating _____   **Your new response** _____

43. Scholarly teachers know that people learn in diverse ways; hence they know that instruction should be diverse as well.

MDN   6.0   IQR 1.0   Your previous rating _____   **Your new response** _____

44. Learning to pose questions about teaching and learning is a starting point in the scholarship of teaching; gathering evidence, interpreting it, sharing results, and changing practice continue the process.

MDN   6.0   IQR 1.0   Your previous rating _____   **Your new response** _____

45. The scholarship of teaching entails a public account of some or all of the following aspects of teaching: vision, design, interaction, outcomes, and analysis—in a manner that can be peer reviewed and used by members of one's community.

MDN   7.0   IQR 1.0   Your previous rating _____   **Your new response** _____

46. Scholarly teachers use assignments and assessments that emphasize higher-order thinking and cognitive skills and relate concepts to real life.

MDN   6.0   IQR 2.25   Your previous rating _____   **Your new response** _____

47. A person practicing the scholarship of teaching is aware of, experiences and can express an underpinning conceptual framework for their teaching, a framework that is strongly related to students' learning outcomes.

MDN   5.5   IQR 1.0   Your previous rating _____   **Your new response** _____

48. The notion of the scholarship of teaching implies that teachers come up with ways to involve students in their own learning.

MDN   4.5   IQR 1.5   Your previous rating _____   **Your new response** _____

Part II

Question: Which, if any, are the issues surrounding the scholarship of teaching that you consider to be unresolved to date?
Directions: For each of the items listed below, please indicate the extent to which you agree or disagree that this is an unresolved issue by assigning a rating between 1 and 7.

Scale

Strongly disagree   1   2   3   4   5   6   7   Strongly agree

1. The lack of broadly acceptable definitions for the *scholarship of teaching, scholarly teaching, excellence in teaching, expert teacher,* and *research on teaching and learning* is an unresolved issue.

MDN   7.0   IQR 1.0   Your previous rating _____   **Your new response** _____

2. The assessment, recognition, and reward of the scholarship of teaching remain primary challenges.

MDN   7.0   IQR 1.0   Your previous rating _____   Your new response _____

3. Who determines the standards and criteria by which to review and critique the scholarship of teaching (learning theorists, cognitive psychologists, discipline specialists) has not been resolved.

MDN   6.0   IQR 1.0   Your previous rating _____   Your new response _____

4. Whether publication of experience and findings in peer-reviewed media is a necessary characteristic of the scholarship of teaching is not clear.

MDN   5.0   IQR 1.0   Your previous rating _____   Your new response _____

5. How the scholarship of teaching is related to the literature on teacher research and action research is not clear.

MDN   5.0   IQR 1.0   Your previous rating _____   Your new response _____

6. The relationship between formal educational research and contextual classroom research remains unclear.

MDN   5.0   IQR 1.0   Your previous rating _____   Your new response _____

7. The lack of an agreed-upon language for communicating about the scholarship of teaching remains a challenge.

MDN   6.0   IQR 2.0   Your previous rating _____   Your new response _____

8. Whether all studies in the scholarship of teaching should be required to include authentic indicators of student learning and development needs to be addressed.

MDN   5.0   IQR 3.0   Your previous rating _____   Your new response _____

9. How to develop a more adequate language to convey legitimacy for the concern with learning outcomes needs to be addressed.

MDN   4.0   IQR 2.0   Your previous rating _____   Your new response _____

10. The role of the faculty development professional in the advancement of pedagogical content knowledge has not been adequately addressed.

MDN   4.0   IQR 2.0   Your previous rating _____   Your new response _____

11. The relationship between the scholarship of discovery on teaching and learning in higher education and the scholarship of teaching has not been adequately addressed (such as whether formal educational research on teaching and learning is a component of the scholarship of teaching).

MDN   5.0   IQR 2.0   Your previous rating _____   Your new response _____

12. Whether and to what extent the scholarship of teaching is something that all academics can successfully practice has not been adequately addressed.

MDN   5.0   IQR 1.0   Your previous rating _____   Your new response _____

13. Whether a scholar of teaching studies teaching as a discipline in itself or through another discipline has not been sufficiently made clear.

MDN   5.0   IQR 2.5   Your previous rating _____   Your new response _____

14. Whether teaching is such a fundamentally local activity that forcing it to become more like peer-reviewed traditional scholarship might corrupt or distort it remains unclear.

MDN   5.0   IQR 4.0   Your previous rating _____   Your new response _____

15. The isolation of the scholarship of teaching from the primary work of the disciplines and of departments is unresolved.

MDN   5.5   IQR 2.25   Your previous rating _____   Your new response _____

16. It remains unclear whether being professional about teaching is the same as being a scholar of teaching.

MDN   4.0   IQR 4.0   Your previous rating _____   Your new response _____

17. The integration of research on teaching and the practice of teaching is not addressed.

MDN   5.0   IQR 2.25   Your previous rating _____   Your new response _____

18. There is confusion about whether anyone who teaches is automatically a scholar of teaching.

MDN   2.0   IQR 3.0   Your previous rating _____   Your new response _____

19. How to cultivate local systems of support for the scholarship of teaching is an unresolved issue.

MDN   5.0   IQR 1.0   Your previous rating _____   Your new response _____

20. How the new technologies of instruction may influence the development of a scholarship of teaching remains an unresolved issue.

MDN   6.0   IQR 2.0   Your previous rating _____   Your new response _____

21. The lack of formal training for faculty on teaching and learning and faculty's resistance to such learning remains an unresolved issue.

MDN   6.0   IQR 2.0   Your previous rating _____   Your new response _____

22. The attainment of the scholarship of teaching is not addressed.

MDN   4.0   IQR 2.5   Your previous rating _____   Your new response _____

23. How to develop communities of discourse around the scholarship of teaching remains an unresolved issue.

MDN   5.0   IQR 3.0   Your previous rating _____   Your new response _____

24. Whether teaching, in order to be valued in the academy, has to be scholarly and whether excellent teaching is not valuable in itself remain unresolved issues.

MDN   4.0   IQR 3.0   Your previous rating _____   Your new response _____

25. Whether student ratings of instruction are acceptable measures of the scholarship of teaching is an unresolved issue.

MDN   2.0   IQR 1.0   Your previous rating _____   Your new response _____

26. The problem that good teaching evaluations are associated with lenient evaluation and are hence misinterpreted by those who use the data remains unresolved.

MDN   2.0   IQR 4.0   Your previous rating _____   Your new response _____

27. Whether being an expert teacher is the same as being a scholar of teaching is an unresolved issue.

MDN   5.0   IQR 3.5   Your previous rating _____   Your new response _____

28. It remains unclear how to build the scholarship of teaching into graduate education.

MDN   6.0   IQR 2.0   Your previous rating _____   Your new response _____

29. The nature of the relationship between the scholarship of teaching and the other three Boyer scholarships is unclear.

MDN   3.0   IQR 5.0   Your previous rating _____   Your new response _____

30. The links between expertise in teaching and expertise in the scholarship of teaching have not been sufficiently explored.

MDN   6.0   IQR 1.5   Your previous rating _____ Your new response _____

31. How teachers can acquire the knowledge and skills to become more scholarly in teaching (here: knowing how to involve students in higher-order learning) has not been adequately addressed.

MDN   5.0   IQR 1.0   Your previous rating _____ Your new response _____

32. Finding adequate approaches for identifying, codifying, reporting, and communicating the wisdom of practice remains a challenge.

MDN   6.0   IQR 2.0   Your previous rating _____ Your new response _____

Are there any issues surrounding the scholarship of teaching that you consider to be unresolved to date that were not mentioned in the first Delphi round or that you feel were not represented accurately in this summary?

Yes_____   (please specify)   No_____

Part III

Directions: For each of the items listed below, please indicate the extent to which you agree or disagree with the statement by assigning a rating between 1 and 7.

Scale

Strongly disagree   1   2   3   4   5   6   7   Strongly agree

1. There is insufficient documentation of teaching and lack of criteria to distinguish excellent from mediocre teaching, let alone the same differentiation for the scholarship of teaching.

MDN   6.0   IQR 4.0   Your previous rating _____ Your new response _____

2. We need careful analysis of the meaning behind the words *expert teacher, scholarly teacher,* and *practicing the scholarship of teaching.*

MDN   6.0   IQR 2.0   Your previous rating _____ Your new response _____

3. Not all teaching is or should be scholarly; people on tenure and promotion committees, or faculty being considered for promotion and tenure, need to understand that.

MDN   5.0   IQR 4.0   Your previous rating _____ Your new response _____

4. Graduate education must change to feature multiple kinds of scholarship.

MDN   6.0   IQR 1.0   Your previous rating _____ Your new response _____

5. By requiring all teachers to practice the scholarship of teaching, we create just another way of devaluing teaching that does not result in publications and similar peer-reviewed documents.

MDN   3.0   IQR 4.0   Your previous rating _____ Your new response _____

6. The scholarship of teaching is being used as a way to upgrade the importance of teaching in higher education and to make it more competitive with research. While this is indeed important, it cannot be the major impetus behind developing a concept of scholarship in teaching.

MDN   5.0   IQR 3.0   Your previous rating _____ Your new response _____

7. Faculty must be educated in how to think of teaching as scholarship (teaching includes software design, course and curriculum development, textbook writing, the development of new approaches to teaching, and so on).

MDN   6.0   IQR 2.0   Your previous rating _____ Your new response _____

8. Faculty must be educated in developing the needed documentation in order to assess the scholarship of teaching.

MDN   6.0   IQR 2.0   Your previous rating _____ Your new response _____

9. Faculty development needs to focus on examples of the scholarship of teaching that are emerging in many disciplines.

MDN   6.0   IQR 2.0   Your previous rating _____ Your new response _____

10. We place too much emphasis on rewarding performance (such as how well someone lectures) rather than enhancement of learning.

MDN   5.0   IQR 3.0   Your previous rating _____ Your new response _____

11. As there is no effective means of assessing the scholarship of teaching, what are needed are representative well-defined and generally accepted forms in which to present the processes and products of the scholarly acts of teaching—forms that can be subjected to peer review.

MDN   6.0   IQR 3.0   Your previous rating _____ Your new response _____

12. Excellence in teaching needs to be valued even if it does not contribute to the scholarship of teaching.

MDN   6.0   IQR 1.0   Your previous rating _____ Your new response _____

13. We need to understand how scholarship of teaching is acquired; the expertise literature could be helpful.

MDN   5.0   IQR 2.0   Your previous rating _____ Your new response _____

14. One can be professional about teaching without being a scholar of teaching. ($n = 10$)

MDN   5.5   IQR 2.5   Your previous rating _____ Your new response _____

15. The scholarship of teaching is practiced by those who engage in formal educational research (discovery research) on teaching and learning in higher education.

MDN   4.0   IQR 4.0   Your previous rating _____ Your new response _____

16. Faculty are without the language to talk about teaching and particularly the scholarship of teaching. Hence they cannot develop discourse that enables them to address teaching and learning in their particular discipline.

MDN   5.0   IQR 2.0   Your previous rating _____ Your new response _____

17. As teaching is a fundamentally local activity, forcing teaching to become similar to peer-reviewed traditional scholarship distorts teaching.

MDN   2.0   IQR 3.0   Your previous rating _____ Your new response _____

18. There is not systemic support for the scholarship of teaching as there is for the scholarship of discovery (that is, the commitment of intellectual energy that goes into the scholarship of teaching, including communication and interactions with colleagues, locally, nationally, and internationally, is rarely acknowledged).

MDN   6.0   IQR 2.0   Your previous rating _____ Your new response _____

19. Too little thought is given to data collection and indicators of impact. ($n = 10$)

MDN   5.5   IQR 2.25   Your previous rating _____ Your new response _____

20. Strong faculty support is needed to value teaching and the scholarship associated with it. Eventually this demand for recognition and reward has to translate into policy.

MDN   6.0   IQR 1.0   Your previous rating _____ Your new response _____

21. New faculty need to be encouraged to become involved in and to support the scholarship of teaching.

MDN   6.0   IQR 2.0   Your previous rating _____ Your new response _____

22. An expert teacher is the same as a scholar of teaching.

MDN   3.0   IQR 4.0   Your previous rating _____ Your new response _____

23. Demonstrating excellence in teaching is the same as practicing the scholarship of teaching.

MDN   3.0   IQR 3.0   Your previous rating _____ **Your new response** _____

24. Every faculty member who teaches is a scholar of teaching.

MDN   1.0   IQR 0   Your previous rating _____ **Your new response** _____

25. In order to rise to the level of scholarly inquiry, faculty members exploring the teaching and learning process cannot rely exclusively on classroom research methods but need to add other research methodologies.

MDN   6.0   IQR 2.0   Your previous rating _____ **Your new response** _____

Exhibit 1.2. Important Features or Components of the Scholarship of Teaching (Part I of the Delphi Questionnaire) Identified by Panelists

Category 1: High Agreement and Strong Group Consensus (MDN = 6.0–7.0; IQR = 0–1.5)

Subcategory 1 (MDN = 6.0–7.0; IQR = 0–0.5)

2. Those who practice the scholarship of teaching carefully design ways to examine, interpret, and share learning about teaching. Thereby, they contribute to the scholarly community of their discipline.
21. Faculty that practice the scholarship of teaching are curious about the ways in which students learn and the effects of certain practices on that learning.
32. The scholarship of teaching has characteristics that make it different from other forms of scholarship, but it also has characteristics that encompass the dimensions of the scholarship of discovery, integration, and application.
41. Engaging in classroom research is important but is not sufficient for the scholarship of teaching.

Subcategory 2 (MDN 6.0–7.0; IQR = 1.0)

23. For people who practice the scholarship of teaching, teaching is driven by an inquiry ethic.
36. Scholarly teachers are always learning both about knowledge in their field and how to make connections with students.
43. Scholarly teachers know that people learn in diverse ways; hence, they know that instruction should be diverse as well.
44. Learning to pose questions about teaching and learning is a starting point in the scholarship of teaching; gathering evidence, interpreting it, sharing results, and changing practice continue the process.
45. The scholarship of teaching entails a public account of some or all of the following aspects of teaching: vision, design, interaction, outcomes, and analysis, in a manner that can be peer reviewed and used by members of one's community.

Subcategory 3 (MDN = 6.0–7.0, IQR = 1.25–1.5)

1. A key feature in the scholarship of teaching is having an understanding of how people learn, knowing what practices are most effective, and having knowledge about what we have learned about teaching.
6. The conduct of research on teaching and learning (less formal and formal) contributes to the advancement of pedagogical content knowledge and presents forms of the scholarship of discovery that overlap with, and are part of, the scholarship of teaching.
9. The scholarship of teaching involves constant reflection of the process and outcomes of teaching and learning and acknowledges the contextual nature of teaching.

13. People practicing the scholarship of teaching focus on change; they develop their practice through a cycle of action, reflection, and improvement.

15. People practicing the scholarship of teaching need to have assessment, evaluation, and research skills. They need to be able to conduct classroom research and document the process of teaching and learning and student progress.

18. The scholarship of teaching is an activity that, in the context of promoting student learning, meets each of the following criteria:

- Requires high levels of discipline-related expertise
- Breaks new ground and is innovative
- Can be replicated and elaborated
- Can be documented
- Can be peer reviewed
- Has significance or impact

20. People practicing the scholarship of teaching make a deliberate effort to share their experience with others (they act as mentors, communicators, faculty developers, etc.).

39. Individuals practicing the scholarship of teaching investigate the relationship between teaching and learning.

40. People who practice the scholarship of teaching generate new ideas about teaching.

Category 2: Lower Agreement and Strong Group Consensus (MDN = 5.0–5.5; IQR = 0.5–1.5)

4. The key features of the scholarship of teaching are content knowledge in the deepest sense and knowledge of pedagogy in the broadest sense, resulting in pedagogical content knowledge.

38. A key feature in the scholarship of teaching is the hard intellectual work that goes into preparing effective learning experiences for students.

47. A person practicing the scholarship of teaching is aware of, experiences, and can express an underpinning conceptual framework for their teaching, a framework that is strongly related to students' learning outcomes.

Exhibit 1.3. Unresolved Issues Surrounding the Scholarship of Teaching (Part II of the Delphi Questionnaire) Identified by Panelists ($n = 10$)

Category 1: High Agreement and Strong Group Consensus (MDN = 6.0–7.0; IQR = 0.5–1.5)

1. The lack of broadly acceptable definitions for the *scholarship of teaching, scholarly teaching, excellence in teaching, expert teacher,* and *research on teaching and learning* is an unresolved issue.

2. The assessment, recognition, and reward of the scholarship of teaching remains a primary challenge.

3. Who determines the standards and criteria by which to review and critique the scholarship of teaching (learning theorists, cognitive psychologists, discipline specialists) has not been resolved.

7. The lack of an agreed-upon language for communicating about the scholarship of teaching remains a challenge.

20. How the new technologies of instruction may influence the development of a scholarship of teaching remains an unresolved issue.

30. The links between expertise in teaching and expertise in the scholarship of teaching have not been sufficiently explored.

Category 2: Lower Agreement and Strong Group Consensus (MDN = 5.0; IQR = 1.0–1.25)

5. How the scholarship of teaching is related to the literature on teacher research and action research is not clear.
6. The relationship between formal educational research and contextual classroom research remains unclear.
12. Whether and to what extent the scholarship of teaching is something that all academics can successfully practice has not been adequately addressed.
13. Whether a scholar of teaching studies teaching as a discipline in itself or whether teaching is studied through another discipline has not been sufficiently made clear.
19. How to cultivate local systems of support for the scholarship of teaching is an unresolved issue.
31. How teachers can acquire the knowledge and skills to become more scholarly in teaching (here: knowing how to involve students in higher order learning) has not been adequately addressed.

Category 3: High Agreement and Lower Group Consensus (MDN = 6.0–7.0; IQR = 2.0–2.25)

21. The lack of formal training for faculty on teaching and learning and faculty's resistance to such learning remains an unresolved issue.
28. It remains unclear how to build the scholarship of teaching into graduate education.
32. Finding adequate approaches for identifying, codifying, reporting, and communicating the wisdom of practice remains a challenge.

Category 4: Lower Agreement and Lower Group Consensus (MDN = 4.5–5.0; IQR = 2.0–2.75)

4. Whether publication of experience or findings in peer-reviewed media is a necessary characteristic of the scholarship of teaching is not clear.
8. Whether all studies in the scholarship of teaching should be required to include authentic indicators of student learning and development needs to be addressed.
11. The relationship between scholarship of discovery on teaching and learning in higher education and the scholarship of teaching has not been adequately addressed (e.g., the question whether formal educational research on teaching and learning is a component of the scholarship of teaching).
15. The isolation of the scholarship of teaching from the primary work of the disciplines and of departments is unresolved.
23. How to develop communities of discourse around the scholarship of teaching remains an unresolved issue.
27. Whether being an expert teacher is the same as being a scholar of teaching is an unresolved issue.

References

Boyer, E. L. *Scholarship Reconsidered: Priorities of the Professoriate.* Princeton, N.J.: Carnegie Foundation for the Advancement of Teaching, 1990.

Clayton, M. J. "Delphi: A Technique to Harness Expert Opinion for Critical Decision-Making Tasks in Education." *Educational Psychology,* 1997, 17, 273–287.

Edgerton, R., Hutchings, P., and Quinlan, K. *The Teaching Portfolio: Capturing the Scholarship of Teaching.* Washington, D.C.: American Association for Higher Education, 1991.

Fish, L. S., and Busby, D. M. "The Delphi Method." In D. H. Sprenkle and S. M. Spoon (eds.), *Research Methods in Family Therapy*. New York: Guilford Press, 1996.

Glassick, C. E., Huber, M. T., and Maeroff, G. I. *Scholarship Assessed: Evaluation of the Professoriate*. San Francisco: Jossey-Bass, 1997.

Kreber, C. "Defining and Implementing the Scholarship of Teaching: The Results of a Delphi Study." Paper presented at the annual meeting of the Canadian Society for the Study of Higher Education, Université de Sherbrooke, Sherbrooke, Quebec, June 1999.

Kreber, C. "Controversy and Consensus on the Scholarship of Teaching," forthcoming.

Kreber, C., and Associates. "Defining and Implementing the Scholarship of Teaching." Symposium at the annual meeting of the American Educational Research Association (Division J), New Orleans, Apr. 2000.

Linstone, H. A., and Turoff, M. *The Delphi Method: Techniques and Applications*. Reading, Mass.: Addison-Wesley, 1975.

Menges, R. J., Weimer, M., and Associates. *Teaching on Solid Ground: Using Scholarship to Improve Practice*. San Francisco: Jossey-Bass, 1995.

Paulsen, M. B., and Feldman, K. A. "Toward a Reconceptualization of Scholarship: A Human Action System with Functional Imperatives." *Journal of Higher Education*, 1995, *66*, 615–641.

Richlin, L. (ed.). *Preparing Faculty for New Conceptions of Scholarship*. New Directions for Teaching and Learning, no. 54. San Francisco: Jossey-Bass, 1993.

Shulman, L. S. "Course Anatomy: The Dissection and Analysis of Knowledge Through Teaching." In P. Hutchings (ed.), *The Course Portfolio: How Faculty Can Examine Their Teaching to Advance Practice and Improve Student Learning*. Washington, D.C.: American Association for Higher Education, 1998.

CAROLIN KREBER is associate professor of adult and higher education in the Department of Educational Policy Studies at the University of Alberta.

2

This chapter examines the relation between research and the scholarship of teaching, with an emphasis on the central role of the creation of pedagogical content knowledge.

The Relation Between Research and the Scholarship of Teaching

Michael B. Paulsen

The conception of scholarship as a distinguishing feature of faculty work has been substantially broadened during the 1990s to include the several distinct, yet interrelated and overlapping, dimensions of discovery (research), integration, application (service), and teaching (Boyer, 1990; Paulsen and Feldman, 1995; Rice, 1992). A growing number of institutions and a variety of disciplinary and professional associations have responded by reconsidering the diverse elements of faculty work, providing a multidimensional view of the scholarly features of such work, and devising general standards or criteria for evaluating the several dimensions of scholarly work in which faculty engage (Diamond and Adam, 1995; Glassick, Huber, and Maeroff, 1997; Hutchings and Shulman, 1999).

The Scholarship of Teaching: In Search of a Definition in the Literature

What constitutes the scholarship of teaching? Before we address the relation between research and the scholarship of teaching, in this section and the next we present the definition of scholarship of teaching that is used as a basis for examining its relation to research throughout the rest of the chapter. The expanding literature on the subject continues to advance us toward a clearer understanding of the nature and meaning of the scholarship of teaching (Cross and Steadman, 1996; Hutchings and Shulman, 1999; Kreber, 1999; Kreber and Cranton, 1997, 2000; Paulsen, 1999; Rice, 1992; Richlin, 1993; Shulman, 1987; Weimer, 1995). Although we have not yet established a common language for articulating the construct, a good deal of productive thinking and writing about it has already occurred, and a consensus is beginning to emerge.

Rice (1992) proposed that the scholarship of teaching is based on the development and application of its several distinct elements: "synoptic capacity," "what we know about learning," and "pedagogical content knowledge" (p. 125). Synoptic capacity is similar to what Shulman (1987) has called *content knowledge,* "scholarship in the content disciplines" (p. 8). The expression "what we know about learning" refers to an element of scholarship that is similar to what Shulman has called "formal educational scholarship," especially about "teaching and learning" (p. 10), and is one of the distinguishing characteristics of what Kreber and Cranton (1997) refer to as *pedagogical knowledge,* "knowledge about how to best facilitate student learning" (p. 5). And finally, *pedagogical content knowledge* "represents the blending of content and pedagogy into an understanding of how particular topics, problems, or issues are organized, represented, and adapted to the diverse interests and abilities of learners, and presented for instruction" (Shulman, 1987, p. 8), or more succinctly, as "knowledge about the interaction between learning process and academic content" (Ronkowski, 1993, p. 80).

The Central Role of Pedagogical Content Knowledge

Pedagogical content knowledge can be viewed as the knowledge that stands at the nexus between content and pedagogical knowledge. Not merely the summation of the two parts, pedagogical content knowledge represents a special synthesis and unique relation of the two. Serving as the substantive and syntactical foundation for the scholarship of teaching, it provides the symbols, language, ideas, concepts, theories, metaphors, analogies, and other forms of knowledge representation, as well as the modes of inquiry, that constitute the knowledge base for effective teaching and learning. Those actions of teachers that result in the creation, construction, or advancement of the pedagogical content knowledge base possess the four characteristics that Hutchings and Shulman (1999) identify as the distinguishing features of acts that constitute the scholarship of teaching: they are available in a form that can be made public to a community of professional peers; they can be evaluated by those peers; they can serve as the basis for future work by the members of that community; and they involve inquiry about teaching and learning. In other words, the domain of pedagogical content knowledge serves as an expanding, ever-changing repository of the symbolic patterns that are created by and inform the discourse, action, substance, and syntax that constitute the scholarship of teaching. Furthermore, scholarly contributions to pedagogical content knowledge can arise from the practice of, reflection on, and codification of teaching (Kreber and Cranton, 1997); faculty evaluation and development (Paulsen, 1999); the content and pedagogical training of graduate students as new faculty (Boyer, 1990; Richlin, 1993); and through the conduct of research on teaching and learning—including both traditional educational research and contextual classroom research (Cross, 1998; Cross and Steadman, 1996; Paulsen, 1999).

Research and the Scholarship of Teaching

The purpose of this chapter is to examine one of the unresolved issues in the study of the scholarship of teaching: the relation between research and the scholarship of teaching. Therefore, we focus on the fourth of the forms of contribution to the creation of pedagogical content knowledge identified earlier: conducting research on teaching and learning. In their earliest writings on the subject of expanding the conception of scholarship, Boyer (1990) and Rice (1992) made their understanding of the construct quite clear: "While we want to treat the four forms of scholarship as individually distinctive, we also want them to be understood as interrelated and often overlapping—an interdependent whole, with each distinctive form encompassing each of the other three" (Rice, p. 125).

In a recent report on their excellent work with members of the Carnegie Academy for the Scholarship of Teaching and Learning, Hutchings and Shulman (1999) carry forth this original viewpoint, but they also emphasize what they see as a substantial relationship between research and the scholarship of teaching: "A scholarship of teaching . . . requires a kind of 'going meta,' in which faculty frame and systematically investigate questions related to student learning—the conditions under which it occurs, what it looks like, how to deepen it, and so forth—and do so with an eye not only to improving their own classroom but to advancing practice beyond it" (p. 13). The conduct of research on teaching and learning, ranging from less formal, context-specific classroom research to more formal, and often more generalizable, traditional educational research, contributes to the advancement of pedagogical content knowledge and represents a form of the scholarship of discovery that overlaps with, and should be viewed as part of, the scholarship of teaching.

Writers in this field are advancing toward consensus on the view that classroom research is one way to engage in the scholarship of teaching (Cross, 1998; Cross and Steadman, 1996; Kreber and Cranton, 1997; Paulsen, 1999; Weimer, 1995). However, for nearly ten years, the progenitors of the popular and effective classroom-research approach to enhancing learning and teaching, Cross and Angelo (1988), used the terms *classroom research* and *classroom assessment* more or less interchangeably, thereby training faculty and faculty developers everywhere to think of classroom research, in a somewhat narrow sense, as referring to the use of a set of classroom assessment techniques (CATs). Today, CATs continue to be valuable tools in the conduct of classroom research. However, it is very important to note that, in her latest work, Cross (1998; Cross and Steadman, 1996) has made a clear and strong conceptual distinction between classroom *assessment* and classroom *research*.

"At first, we used the terms *Classroom Assessment* and *Classroom Research* almost interchangeably, but we are now beginning to stress important distinctions between them. Classroom Assessment usually addresses the status quo or 'what' questions of teaching and learning. . . . Classroom Research, in contrast, usually addresses understanding—the 'why' and 'how' questions about learning. . . . Broadly speaking, Classroom Research attempts to provide some insight into *how* students learn" (Cross, 1998, p. 8).

Of particular relevance here is that Cross and Steadman have also made a special effort to point out that classroom research, as it is now conceptually distinguished from classroom assessment, is characterized as "scholarly" because "it builds upon the knowledge base of [traditional] research on teaching and learning" (Cross and Steadman, 1996, p. 3). In fact, one of the expressed purposes of their book *Classroom Research: Implementing the Scholarship of Teaching* is to provide a resource to help faculty "to integrate their firsthand teaching experience with recent research and theory on learning" (p. xii). In other words, their new conceptualization of classroom research views it as a form of research that is solidly grounded in, well informed by, and interdependent with the existing knowledge base of traditional theory and research on teaching and learning. Cross first articulated this view in her earlier work with Angelo (1988, p. 384) as follows:

> While much of the work . . . will continue the well-formulated pattern of Classroom Assessment, we note the continuing hunger for deeper understanding of the complexities of learning. This need is recognized in the implied promise of the name *Classroom Research*. The expectation is that research conducted in the classroom will advance knowledge about learning. Without question, Classroom Assessment can advance knowledge about a particular situation, . . . whether a given teaching technique works, to what extent it works, and for which students. What Classroom Assessment does not tell us is *why* it works. For that, we need to establish relationships between learning theory and teaching practice.

More recently, Cross and Steadman (1996) summarized the relations among the scholarship of teaching, classroom research, and existing theory and research on teaching and learning in the following manner: "Observing students in the act of learning, reflecting, and discussing observations and data with teaching colleagues, and reading the literature on what is already known about learning is one way teachers can implement the scholarship of teaching. It is what we call *Classroom Research*" (p. 2).

Clearly, the knowledge base of both traditional educational research about teaching and learning and contextual classroom research are important components of the scholarship of teaching. Because of this, it is important to clarify the links between these two perspectives on research about teaching and learning. Cross (1998) explains that "Classroom Research, if it is to be effective, requires the careful launching and testing of insightful hypotheses . . . but it should also be related to broader themes about learning, themes that exist in the [traditional] literature on learning" (p. 11). In other words, the effectiveness of classroom research requires that traditional educational research be substantial, accessible, and ongoing. Therefore, the conduct of traditional or formal educational research constitutes a contribution, at least indirectly, to the scholarship of teaching.

As noted previously, pedagogical content knowledge—the creation of which constitutes an act of scholarship—stands at the nexus between pedagogical and content knowledge. And it is the relation and application of pedagogical knowledge to the facilitation of student learning of content knowledge in a particular disciplinary and classroom context that leads to the creation of pedagogical content knowledge. Fundamentally, pedagogical content knowledge is a discipline- or content-specific knowledge base. Effective classroom research, therefore, requires that teachers be as well informed about the content knowledge produced by traditional disciplinary research as about the pedagogical knowledge produced by traditional educational research (Cross and Steadman, 1996).

Sorting It Out: The Relation of Research and the Scholarship of Teaching

Figure 2.1 illustrates the various relations that exist between research and the scholarship of teaching. Traditional educational research—for example, studies conducted using the substantive and syntactical structures of disciplines such as social, cognitive, developmental, and educational psychology—produces most of our extant pedagogical knowledge, the general principles that inform our understanding of what constitutes effective teaching and learning in the postsecondary setting. This relationship is illustrated in Figure 2.1 by arrow A. In a parallel manner, traditional disciplinary research—studies conducted using the substantive and syntactical structures of specific disciplines—produces the content knowledge that characterizes each of the existing individual disciplinary specializations, a relationship that is illustrated by arrow B.

Scholars of teaching in various fields who are well informed in both the content knowledge of their respective disciplines and the pedagogical knowledge or knowledge of principles of effective teaching and learning that are generalizable across disciplines can integrate or synthesize the two knowledge bases to create pedagogical content knowledge (see Figure 2.1, arrows C and D). The figure illustrates four ways that scholars of teaching can integrate content and pedagogical knowledge to create pedagogical content knowledge: by practicing teaching and reflecting on their experiences (E), by engaging in the activities of faculty evaluation and development (F), by participating in effective programs of graduate training (G), and by conducting classroom research (J). Conducting classroom research is, of course, the one that is most relevant to the relation between research and

Figure 2.1 Research and the Scholarship of Teaching

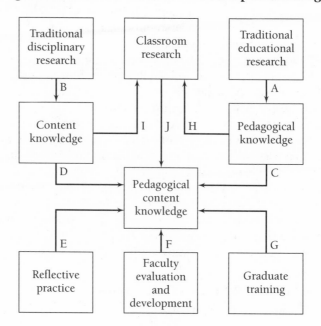

the scholarship of teaching. Because classroom research refers to studies that teachers conduct to investigate how and why students learn in their own particular disciplines and classrooms, the most well-informed classroom research is grounded in the substantive and syntactical structures of both content and pedagogical knowledge (see arrows H and I).

The paths indicated by arrows A-C and A-H-J illustrate the effects of traditional educational research on the creation of pedagogical content knowledge, whereas the paths indicated by arrows B-D and B-I-J illustrate the parallel effects of traditional disciplinary research. As illustrated by path A-C, traditional educational research produces pedagogical knowledge that scholars of teaching, in turn, can use in several ways—in combination with content knowledge—to create pedagogical content knowledge. Path A-H-J highlights the view that the pedagogical knowledge produced by traditional educational research informs the conduct of classroom research that then contributes to the creation of pedagogical content knowledge. In a parallel fashion, path B-D illustrates the view that traditional disciplinary research produces the content knowledge that scholars of teaching, in turn, can combine with pedagogical knowledge in several different ways to create pedagogical content knowledge. And path B-I-J signifies that the content knowledge produced by traditional disciplinary research informs the conduct of classroom research that itself contributes to the creation of pedagogical content knowledge. Finally, the H-J and I-J paths illustrate the view that well-informed classroom research, grounded in the substantive (conceptual) frameworks and syntactical (methodological) structures of both content and pedagogical knowledge, constitutes a direct contribution to the creation of pedagogical content knowledge.

Figure 2.1 illustrates yet another important feature of the relation between research and the scholarship of teaching: the differences between direct and indirect effects. In the figure, path A indicates that traditional educational research has a direct effect on the development of pedagogical knowledge. However, paths A-C and A-H-J indicate that traditional educational research has only an indirect effect on the creation of pedagogical content knowledge, through its effects on pedagogical knowledge and classroom research. Similarly, paths B, B-D, and B-I-J indicate that traditional disciplinary research has a direct effect on the creation of content knowledge, but only an indirect effect on the creation of pedagogical content knowledge, through its effects on content knowledge and classroom research. However, content and pedagogical knowledge themselves—the products of traditional educational and disciplinary research—have direct effects on pedagogical content knowledge, as does the conduct of classroom research that is well informed by both content and pedagogical knowledge.

Conclusions: Comparisons with the Findings of an International Delphi Study of the Scholarship of Teaching

During the past two years, an international panel of experts has served as the foundation for a Delphi study intended to identify the principal features or components of the notion of the scholarship of teaching (Kreber, 1999). The results of the study indicated that the panelists reached high levels of both agreement and consensus about eighteen of forty-eight statements (for a distinction, see Chapter One of this volume). As a form of cross validation of the arguments presented earlier in this chapter, this section presents ten of those eighteen statements, selected for their relevance to the topic of this chapter, arranged in four sets, with a brief comment about how each set corresponds to a different aspect of the chapter's central argument about the relation between research and the scholarship of teaching.

The scholarships of teaching and research overlap:

1. The conduct of research on teaching and learning (less formal and formal) contributes to the advancement of pedagogical content knowledge and presents forms of the scholarship of discovery that overlap with, and are part of, the scholarship of teaching. (Part I, item 6)
2. The scholarship of teaching has characteristics that make it different from other forms of scholarship, but it also has characteristics that encompass the dimensions of the scholarship of discovery, integration, and application. (Part I, item 32)

The first statement synthesizes the argument of this chapter, including this chapter's view that the essential character of scholarly acts of teaching is that they contribute to the advancement of pedagogical content knowledge. The remainder of the first statement, as well as the second statement in this pair, clearly, directly, and explicitly supports the argument posed in this chapter that research on teaching and learning is one feature of the scholarship of teaching; that is, the scholarships of teaching and of discovery (research) overlap in important and meaningful ways (Boyer, 1990; Rice, 1992).

The conduct of research on learning and teaching is a substantial component and distinguishing feature of the scholarship of teaching:

3. Individuals practicing the scholarship of teaching investigate the relationship between teaching and learning. (Part I, item 39)
4. Learning to pose questions about teaching and learning is a starting point in the scholarship of teaching; gathering evidence, interpreting it, sharing results, and changing practice continue the process. (Part I, item 44)
5. Those who practice the scholarship of teaching carefully design ways to examine, interpret, and share learning about teaching. Thereby, they contribute to the scholarly community of their discipline. (Part I, item 2)
6. The scholarship of teaching is an activity that, in the context of promoting student learning, meets each of the following criteria:
   • Requires high levels of discipline-related expertise
   • Breaks new ground and is innovative
   • Can be replicated and elaborated
   • Can be documented
   • Can be peer reviewed
   • Has significance or impact (Part I, item 18)

These four statements represent, with increasing complexity and thoroughness, a fairly straightforward description of the scholarship of teaching as characterized by the familiar steps of the research process. Their common theme is further reinforced because this researchlike view of the scholarship of teaching also appears in the first two statements we examined, which explicitly support the view that the scholarships of teaching and research overlap, and in the next two statements we discuss, which explicitly view classroom research as a component of teaching scholarship. In combination, these are six out of the overall eighteen items about which panelists reached high levels of both agreement and consensus (Kreber, 1999) and is quite consistent with Hutchings and Shulman's description of the most distinctive features of the construct (1999).

The final statement adds further support to this view, indicating that acts of scholarship of teaching must meet a set of criteria that are very similar to those used to assess faculty work in the domain of the scholarship of discovery (Diamond and Adam, 1995).

Content and pedagogical knowledge jointly contribute to pedagogical content knowledge and the scholarship of teaching:

7. Scholarly teachers are always learning both about knowledge in their field and how to make connections with students. (Part I, item 36)
8. A key feature in the scholarship of teaching is having an understanding of how people learn, knowing what practices are most effective, and having knowledge about what we have learned about teaching. (Part I, item 1)

In combination, these two statements clearly identify the pedagogical knowledge produced by traditional educational research and the content knowledge produced by traditional disciplinary research as elements of the scholarship of teaching, supporting a central point of this chapter's argument. By way of their direct contribution to the creation of both pedagogical and content knowledge, traditional educational and disciplinary research have an indirect effect on the creation of pedagogical content knowledge.

Classroom research contributes to pedagogical content knowledge and the scholarship of teaching:

9. People practicing the scholarship of teaching need to have assessment, evaluation, and research skills. They need to be able to conduct classroom research and document the process of teaching and learning and student progress. (Part I, item 15)
10. Engaging in classroom research is important but is not sufficient for the scholarship of teaching. (Part I, item 41)

The first statement in this pair clearly suggests that, among other things, the capacity to conduct classroom research is a necessary condition for the practice of the scholarship of teaching. But the second statement initially appears to contradict it, as well as the general argument presented in this chapter. Because this issue was addressed at some length earlier in this chapter, we review it only briefly here. Between 1986 and 1996, faculty and faculty developers followed Cross and Angelo's practice of using the terms *classroom research* and *classroom assessment* more or less interchangeably. Today, CATs continue to be an important tool in most classroom research projects. However, in her latest writing, Cross (Cross, 1998; Cross and Steadman, 1996) has established a clear and strong conceptual distinction between them: although CATs alone can be used to address the questions of what students learn, classroom research, as reconceptualized by Cross, uses CATs and other methods to address the deeper questions of how and why students learn. The new conceptualization views classroom research as capable of meaningfully addressing these deeper issues because it is solidly grounded in, and well informed by, the existing knowledge base of traditional theory and research on teaching and learning.

Nevertheless, because virtually all writing on the subject of classroom research (with the exceptions of Cross, 1998, and Cross and Steadman, 1996) was devoted to the use of CATs, it seems highly likely that the panelists in the Delphi study interpreted the term *classroom research* just as it has been repeatedly described in the extensive existing literature. Under these circumstances, the high levels of agreement and consensus among panelists on this item would, in all likelihood, mean that classroom assessment or the use of CATs was truly viewed by panelists as not sufficient for the scholarship of teaching, whereas classroom research, as recently reconceptualized by Cross, would have been viewed as sufficient to constitute an act of scholarship of teaching. In combination, these statements support another key point of this chapter's argument: classroom research, well informed by pedagogical and content knowledge, makes a direct contribution to the advancement of pedagogical content knowledge and constitutes an act of scholarship of teaching.

References

Boyer, E. L. *Scholarship Reconsidered: Priorities of the Professoriate.* Princeton, N.J.: Carnegie Foundation for the Advancement of Teaching, 1990.

Cross, K. P. "Classroom Research: Implementing the Scholarship of Teaching." In T. A. Angelo (ed.), *Classroom Assessment and Research: An Update on Uses, Approaches, and Research Findings.* New Directions for Teaching and Learning, no. 75. San Francisco: Jossey-Bass, 1998.

Cross, K. P., and Angelo, T. A. *Classroom Assessment Techniques: A Handbook for Faculty.* Ann Arbor, Mich.: National Center for Research to Improve Postsecondary Teaching and Learning, 1988.

Cross, K. P., and Steadman, M. H. *Classroom Research: Implementing the Scholarship of Teaching.* San Francisco: Jossey-Bass, 1996.

Diamond, R. M., and Adam, B. E. (eds.). *The Disciplines Speak: Rewarding the Scholarly, Professional, and Creative Work of Faculty.* Washington, D.C.: American Association for the Study of Higher Education, 1995.

Glassick, C. E., Huber, M. T., and Maeroff, G. I. *Scholarship Assessed: Evaluation of the Professoriate.* San Francisco: Jossey-Bass, 1997.

Hutchings, P., and Shulman, L. S., "The Scholarship of Teaching: New Elaborations, New Developments." *Change,* Sept.-Oct. 1999, pp. 11–15.

Kreber, C. "Defining and Implementing the Scholarship of Teaching: The Results of a Delphi Study." Paper presented at the annual meeting of the Canadian Society for the Study of Higher Education, Université de Sherbrooke, Sherbrooke, Quebec, June 1999.

Kreber, C., and Cranton, P. A. "Teaching as Scholarship: A Model for Instructional Development." *Issues and Inquiry in College Learning and Teaching,* 1997, 19(2), 4–12.

Kreber, C., and Cranton, P. A. "Exploring the Scholarship of Teaching." *Journal of Higher Education,* 2000, 71, 476–495.

Paulsen, M. B. "How College Students Learn: Linking Traditional Educational Research and Contextual Classroom Research." *Journal of Staff, Program and Organization Development,* 1999, 16(2), 63–71.

Paulsen, M. B., and Feldman, K. A. "Toward a Reconceptualization of Scholarship: A Human Action System with Functional Imperatives." *Journal of Higher Education,* 1995, 66, 615–640.

Rice, E. A. "Toward a Broader Conception of Scholarship: The American Context." In T. G. Whiston, and R. L. Geiger (eds.), *Research and Higher Education in the United Kingdom and the United States.* Lancaster, England: Society for Research into Higher Education, 1992.

Richlin, L. (ed.). *Preparing Faculty for the New Conceptions of Scholarship.* New Directions for Teaching and Learning, no. 54. San Francisco: Jossey-Bass, 1993.

Ronkowski, S. A. "Scholarly Teaching: Developmental Stages of Pedagogical Scholarship." In L. Richlin (ed.), *Preparing Faculty for the New Conceptions of Scholarship.* New Directions for Teaching and Learning, no. 54. San Francisco: Jossey-Bass, 1993.

Shulman, L. S. "Knowledge and Teaching: Foundations of the New Reform." *Harvard Education Review,* 1987, 57, 1–22.

Weimer, M. "Why Scholarship Is the Bedrock of Good Teaching." In R. J. Menges, M. Weimer, and Associates, *Teaching on Solid Ground: Using Scholarship to Improve Practice.* San Francisco: Jossey-Bass, 1995.

MICHAEL B. PAULSEN *is professor of education in the Department of Educational Leadership, Counseling and Foundations at the University of New Orleans.*

3

If teaching and the scholarship it embodies are to be evaluated and valued, then it is critical to define its characteristics and outcomes. Our judgments about teachers, their scholarship, and their teaching require information that can be used to support both formative and summative decisions. Michael Theall discusses formative considerations in Part I, and John A. Centra provides guidelines and criteria for decision making in Part II.

Assessing the Scholarship of Teaching: Valid Decisions from Valid Evidence

Michael Theall, John A. Centra

In this chapter, the focus is on assessing the scholarship of teaching. We consider the available definitions and the results of a recent Delphi study by this volume's editor (Kreber, 1999), and propose what assessment or evaluation data, methods, analyses, interpretations, and conclusions would be appropriate and most likely to result in valid and reliable decisions. We examine how the data collected can support both formative and summative uses, and how the improvement of teaching as a result of such assessment can itself be a documentation of scholarship. We also consider the context in which the scholarship and its assessment take place and make recommendations for practice that meet both technical and practical criteria. We consider instrumental (process) and consequential (outcome) data, and how these different kinds of information can be used effectively to document and establish the scholarship of teaching.

Background

Prior to Boyer's development of the phrase *scholarship of teaching* (1990), there was a distance between teaching and other aspects of faculty life and responsibility. The classic teaching-research-service triad treated the three aspects of faculty performance differently, and evaluation practice at the time suggested that although it was assumed that data for judgments about research and service were both accessible and understandable, information about teaching was more of a problem because it was complex and time intensive. From the mid-1960s, the emphasis on student ratings dramatically increased the amount of use of these data. One important change was initiated in the 1980s when the Canadian Association of University Teachers proposed a teaching dossier (Shore and others, 1986) and this process was popularized by Seldin (1993) in the form of the teaching portfolio. At the same time, interest in the techniques of successful college teaching resulted in several books (for example, Davis, 1993; Ebel, 1977; Lowman, 1984; McKeachie's *Teaching Tips* (1999), now in its tenth edition; and since 1980, the New Directions for Teaching and Learning series). Shulman's development of the concept of *pedagogical content knowledge* (1989), a combination of content expertise and deep understanding of the most effective methods of teaching and learning that content, added to the credibility of teaching as an act that incorporated scholarship. This work was supplemented by the rising importance and acknowledged usefulness of classroom assessment techniques and classroom research for both formative and summative purposes (Cross and Angelo, 1988; Cross and Steadman, 1996). The confluence of these streams of interest and investigation made the discussion of the scholarship of teaching both timely and important.

Definitions

Boyer (1990) said, "The work of the professor becomes consequential only when it is understood by others. When defined as scholarship, however, teaching both educates and entices future scholars" (p. 23). Further, Boyer noted the importance of deeply knowing content, building bridges between the teacher's understanding and the student's learning, carefully planning and examining of pedagogical procedures, stimulating active learning, and going beyond transmitting knowledge to transforming and extending it.

These criteria and explanations served to enliven the discussion, but they did not provide sufficient clarity to be operationally useful in the assessment of the scholarship of teaching. Boyer began his investigation of scholarship in the 1980s, and he was deeply involved in the work leading to the publication of *Scholarship Assessed* (Glassick, Huber, and Maeroff, 1997, for which Boyer also wrote the prologue). Glassick, Huber, and Maeroff propose "that there is a common language in which to discuss the standards for scholarly work of all kinds," and they further identify six standards for scholarly work: "clear goals, adequate preparation, appropriate methods, significant results, effective presentation, and reflective critique," noting that these six criteria are "appropriate to the full range of scholarly work" (p. 35).

The authors further explain each criterion through a short series of general questions. But are these criteria and attendant questions sufficient to allow the valid and reliable assessment of teaching as scholarship? On the one hand, there is a problem because the questions in the list are phrased only in terms of the teacher-scholar. For example, with respect to the criterion of significant results, the question is "Does the scholar achieve the goals?" (Glassick, Huber, and Maeroff, 1997, p. 36). In an instructional setting, this language does not sufficiently distinguish between *instructional goals,* the instructor's targets of accomplishment, and *instructional objectives,* the targets of accomplishment set for, with, and sometimes by the students. Too often, the terms are mixed, and the so-called course objectives include only statements of course content or activities, without reference to specific student achievements and the methods used to determine whether these achievements meet prespecified criteria.

This problem can be solved, however, with some translation. *Goals* can be easily changed to *instructional objectives,* and the quality of course design can be judged, in part, by determining whether (1) the objectives are realistic and appropriate; (2) the instructional strategies, activities, assignments, and assessments match the specified objectives; and (3) the course design presents adequate evidence of student learning and achievement of the objectives. Significant results are thus defined in terms of outcomes. With respect to the assessment movement and classroom assessment techniques (Angelo and Cross, 1993), a parallel is found in the use of ongoing classroom assessment for formative purposes, and with respect to outcomes assessment for purposes such as institutional research, program evaluation, and accreditation.

In sum, the application of the principles of *Scholarship Reconsidered* and *Scholarship* Assessed to real-world and now to virtual classrooms requires careful review of the general criteria and the development of more specific standards if reliable and valid measurement of the scholarship of teaching is to take place. In the remainder of this chapter, we explore ways in which to match the methods of investigation to the instructional situations, and we consider how the necessarily varied kinds of information about teaching and learning can be analyzed and reported for best use by decision makers. We also propose a synergy between the evaluation and assessment functions of the investigative processes and the application of findings to instructional improvement and faculty development. Although the goal of evaluation is always to make a judgment of worth, the roles of evaluation in this case are not only to make decisions and to enable improvement but also to identify excellence so that it can be recognized and rewarded.

Part I: Scholarship and Improvement

The experts in Kreber's study (1999) did not agree when asked to rank the five most important components of the scholarship of teaching, nor did they agree about its five most critical unresolved issues.

There was some agreement, however, when the panelists rated each of the items in the two categories. Highly rated items dealt with the need to possess the equivalent of pedagogical content knowledge, with teachers' ongoing reflection and inquiry into the process and outcomes of instruction, with sharing knowledge in formal and informal ways, and with attention to students' needs and individual differences. The panel also agreed that the scholarship of teaching did not require successful grant writing, that being engaged in the work of teaching did not guarantee that a person was a scholar of teaching, and that effective teaching can take place even if the faculty member is not engaged in the formal scholarship of teaching. Finally, the panel agreed that effective teaching and demonstrations of the scholarship of teaching must be valued and supported, and that many faculty need training in the design of effective instruction, the process of classroom research, and the documentation of their efforts.

What does the study tell us about the relationship of scholarship to instructional improvement? Despite the lack of unanimous agreement, what stands out is quite simply that the two must coexist. In a discussion of the evaluation of teaching, Theall and Franklin proposed "a multipurpose system for evaluation, improvement, and research" (1990, p. 31). In this system, theory, research, and practice interact, with the various components constantly informing each other. A similar model is proposed here in Figure 3.1 to demonstrate the important and necessary synergy between the scholarship of teaching and the improvement of teaching.

In Figure 3.1, current scholarship from three general areas is represented within the circles. The italicized terms are typical contributions of the research to day-to-day practice. For example, the literatures of research, evaluation, and assessment provide processes for data collection and analysis. The central triangle represents day-to-day teaching practice, which is informed by the research, theory from the circles, and the disciplinary specialty and practical experience. The bidirectional arrows indicate that scholarship of teaching involves both the use of existing research and theory and the contribution of new understanding through the application of scholarly process to day-to-day practice. Improvement comes about through the teachers' investigation of specific teaching and learning contexts, and this process adds to pedagogical content knowledge by incorporating important factors in teaching and learning across disciplines. Thus one way to improve practice is to carry out classroom research (Cross and Steadman, 1996), which contributes to the realms of research and theory as well as to better understanding of the immediate context.

This research is brought back to practice in two ways: by the direct contributions of faculty who carry out the classroom research and by the work of instructional design and faculty development practitioners who help faculty to enhance instructional effectiveness and to improve learning. When faculty participate in this cycle, they use skills from the arena of the scholarship of discovery, which, according to Boyer (1990), is aimed at the production of knowledge in a given field through research. They bring together information from varied sources and integrate it into the perspectives of their disciplines and classrooms. They apply it to their own and others' teaching and learning situations. And in doing all this, faculty demonstrate the scholarship of teaching.

Collaboration. The literature of instructional consultation (for example, Brinko and Menges, 1997) has concentrated on the interactions of faculty and professionals in instructional design and development for the

Figure 3.1. Scholarship-Improvement-Practice Synergy

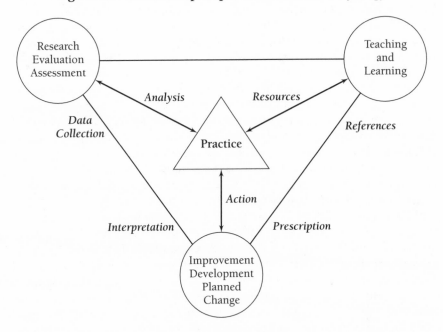

specific purpose of improving teaching and learning. A broader view (for example, Schuster, Wheeler, and Associates, 1990) includes faculty development issues such as professional growth, career development, and faculty vitality. When we combine these complementary views, the cast of players involved in the scholarship of teaching increases because instructional improvement can be combined with exploration and investigation of teaching and learning phenomena. These efforts can and should include evaluation and assessment processes; thus professionals in these areas can also be partners in efforts to better understand and explain what happens in and out of classrooms. An additional benefit is that what we learn in such efforts is important and meaningful to institutional research and other needs of departments, colleges, and universities.

In Kreber's study (1999), panelists differed about the extent to which the public presentation and dissemination of information and knowledge were part of the scholarship of teaching (see Chapter Five of this volume). An additional benefit of institutional collaborations is that they enlarge the array and accessibility of forums for disseminating what is learned in classroom studies, assessment, activities, evaluations, or other joint efforts to gather and use information. The professional organizations of the participants in collaborative efforts are often more receptive to presentations on pedagogy than are disciplinary associations that focus on research specific to the discipline's own body of knowledge.

Increasing the range of opportunities to present and discuss one's pedagogical knowledge, process, or findings has two benefits for faculty development. First, there is direct benefit to those who present or publish results. Second, but equally important, collaborative efforts bring the life of the classroom into the day-to-day reach and attention of units and individuals across campus and reinforce the notion that, rather than being in a closed society apart from the academic community, they are partners with the rest of the institutional community in achieving excellence. Their work supports and is supported by what others learn and share. The scholarship of teaching thus becomes the scholarship of the institution, and it is inclusive and meaningful rather than separate and unrelated to practice.

Practical and Contextual Concerns. The scholarship of teaching is not a concept, a practice, an idea that can exist in a vacuum. Making it so would return the scholar to a lonely ivory tower and put distance between scholarship and practice, between scholars and the real academic world of teachers and learners. The implications are that the scholarship of teaching requires time and emphasis on shared visions, shared efforts, and shared accomplishments. Are there practical limitations? The answer must be yes. Institutional size, mission, history, resources, and vitality all play a part. A small liberal arts college dedicated to teaching and learning may have an environment suitable to furthering the scholarship of teaching but may not have resources to support dissemination. Conversely, a large research-intensive institution may have many resources but focus on traditional research in the disciplines and a reward structure that does not reward the scholarship of teaching. The dynamics within departments differ widely and may affect levels of faculty interest and involvement, and the nature of differences across disciplines may impact at the department or even college level (for example, see Hativa and Marincovich, 1995; Smart and Feldman, 1998).

This kind of situational variety makes it difficult to propose a standard process or set of criteria that can be used to assess the quality or importance of the scholarship of teaching. Like any other complex endeavor, it has many components, and these form a whole greater than the sum of the parts. To exhibit all the qualities of one who is engaged in the scholarship of teaching, a teacher must have time, talent, technique, and training. For this reason, it is imperative for institutions to establish supportive conditions and to actively recognize and reward those who make it part of their professional and academic lives to inquire into and to contribute to our understanding of the dynamic and multidimensional constructs we call teaching and learning.

Part II: Criteria and Sources of Information

The scholarship of teaching can exist at the level of the individual teacher, the department, or the institution. Assessment of this scholarship must therefore be conducted at each of these levels. The important features or components of the scholarship of teaching as identified by the panel (see

Exhibits 1.1 and 1.2) can be grouped into three areas: (1) a shared public account of teaching, (2) an emphasis on learning outcomes and relevant teaching practices, and (3) discipline and pedagogical knowledge and innovation. I identified these three areas or dimensions by grouping the items that the panel of experts agreed were significant.

To assess the scholarship of teaching for each of the three areas, I first identified criteria in the form of questions. Each set of criteria relates to scholarship at the individual, the department, or the institutional level. Next, I identified the sources of information or methods of evaluation for the criteria. By so doing, I present a template that allows valid decisions to be made about the scholarship of teaching. The three areas or dimensions of the scholarship of teaching, along with specified items that illustrate the dimension, follow. I list examples of criteria or questions under the three levels (individual teacher, department, and institution).

Shared Public Account of Teaching

2. Those who practice the scholarship of teaching carefully design ways to examine, interpret, and share learning about teaching. Thereby, they contribute to the scholarly community of their discipline.

45. The scholarship of teaching entails a public account of some or all of the following aspects of teaching: vision, design, interaction, outcomes, and analysis, in a manner that can be peer reviewed and used by members of one's community.

20. People practicing the scholarship of teaching make a deliberate effort to share their experience with others (they act as mentors, communicators, faculty developers, etc.).

Individual Teacher Level. We can identify several criteria that help determine whether the person practices a shared public account of teaching. Does the teacher

- Invite colleagues into his or her class to gain their reactions?
- Visit colleagues' classes to offer useful suggestions?
- Prepare publicly available course outlines and examinations that reflect course objectives, instructional methods, and expected student learning?
- Talk about course content, teaching, or students with colleagues at lunch or other informal gatherings?
- Invite discussions with faculty development or other advisors (for example, media, computer, or testing specialists)?
- Discuss new findings in the discipline with colleagues?
- Show a willingness to share or discuss publicly his or her student evaluations?
- Mentor students or young colleagues on teaching or research activities?
- Participate in conferences, workshops, and seminars on teaching and learning?
- Write articles on teaching or student learning?

Department Level. Criteria to help assess the extent to which a shared public account of teaching exists at this level include the following. Does the department

- Have a system for peer review of teaching?
- Encourage discussion of teaching and course content topics at department meetings?
- Encourage or require members to prepare a teaching portfolio or self-report that describes instructional objectives and vision, teaching methods, learning outcomes, and other aspects of teaching?
- Have a mentoring system for junior faculty that includes teaching as well as research performance?
- Encourage classroom visits and other means of fostering informal discussions of teaching?
- Make public department-level student evaluations of teaching?
- Support faculty attendance at conferences or workshops on teaching and learning?

Institutional Level. The following criteria help determine whether the institution reflects a shared public account of teaching. Does it

- Support an active faculty development or teaching and learning program?
- Have a public policy that encourages the use of student and colleague evaluations?
- Support a mentoring program for junior teachers?
- Support a training program for teaching assistants?
- Weight teaching performance heavily in personnel selection and promotion?
- Sponsor seminars or workshops on teaching and learning?
- Encourage or require faculty to construct a teaching portfolio or a detailed report on teaching?
- Have a policy of periodic review of teaching for tenured and nontenured faculty?
- Publish results of learning outcomes and teaching environment surveys?

Emphasis on Learning Outcomes and Relevant Teaching Practices

21. Faculty who practice the scholarship of teaching are curious about the ways in which students learn and the effects of certain practices on that learning.
43. Scholarly teachers know that people learn in diverse ways; hence, they know that instruction should be diverse as well.
39. Individuals practicing the scholarship of teaching investigate the relationship between teaching and learning.

Other items in this dimension are numbers 15 and 47 (see Exhibit 1.1).

Individual Teacher Level. The following criteria are important as a basis of assessment for an emphasis on learning outcomes and relevant teaching practices. Does the teacher

- Conduct classroom research and use the results to modify teaching?
- Employ a variety of methodologies to supplement or replace lecturing?
- Take into account different student learning styles in designing instruction, exams, and assignments?
- Read extensively about student learning styles and innovations in teaching?
- Discuss classroom research results at seminars or conferences?

Department Level. The criteria listed here are examples of an emphasis on learning outcomes and relevant teaching practices. Does the department

- Administer comprehensive exams in the major field?
- Encourage team teaching or interdisciplinary courses?
- Display openness to innovation in teaching?
- Encourage research on teaching and learning?
- Ask students to include in course or department evaluations their perceptions of learning outcomes as well as the effectiveness of teaching practices?

Institutional Level. The following criteria are examples of an institution's emphasis on learning outcomes and relevant teaching practices. Does the institution

- Support research on learning outcomes and teaching through grants to the faculty?
- Have a testing program across the institution on learning outcomes?
- Survey students and graduates regarding their learning experiences at the institution?
- Survey students and graduates regarding their learning experiences at the institution?
- Emphasize evidence of student learning in personnel decisions?

Discipline and Pedagogical Knowledge and Innovation
4. The key features of the scholarship of teaching are content knowledge in the deepest sense and knowledge of pedagogy in the broadest sense, resulting in pedagogical content knowledge.
36. Scholarly teachers are always learning both about knowledge in their field and how to make connections with students.
1. A key feature in the scholarship of teaching is having an understanding of how people learn, knowing what practices are most effective, and having knowledge about what we have learned about teaching.

Other items in this dimension: 6, 9, 13, 23, 32, 38, 40, and 44 (see Exhibit 1.1).

Individual Teacher Level. The following are criteria for assessing discipline and pedagogical knowledge and innovation. Does the teacher

- Read extensively in the literature of the discipline and on how to connect with students?
- Design courses and assignments that reflect active learning and examinations with real-world applications?
- Design course content that includes a synthesis of new knowledge in the field?
- Encourage students to conduct research or scholarly inquiry in the field?

Department Level. Criteria related to discipline and pedagogical knowledge and innovation include the following. Does the department

- Sponsor seminars or workshops about teaching in the discipline?
- Encourage nontraditional approaches to teaching?
- Reward members who publish or give conference papers on teaching in the discipline?

Institutional Level. The following are criteria to help assess discipline and pedagogical knowledge and innovation. Does the institution

- Emphasize in its reward system not only knowledge of subject content but also effective teaching practice?
- Have a faculty development program with staff committed to working with departments to promote the unique ways in which discipline knowledge may be related to students?
- Have a faculty development program that emphasizes nontraditional teaching practices?

Sources of Information

The following are examples of sources of information that may address the criteria for a scholarship of teaching.

At the individual teacher level, the self-report or teaching portfolio could provide evidence of classroom assessment projects, teaching methodologies, and personal reflections on teaching. Course syllabi should reflect, to some extent, a teacher's knowledge of both the discipline and pedagogy, as well as innovations in teaching. Analyses of assignments and examinations can be a source to identify the quality and quantity of learning. Student and peer evaluations provide another source of information on teaching practices and student perceptions of learning.

Consulting the departmental annual review can be helpful for assessing the extent to which a department exhibits a scholarship of teaching. Although such reviews tend to emphasize faculty workload, publications, and grants, they should also provide evidence on the quality of teaching in the department. Results of major field tests, the Graduate Record Examination, or other senior examinations also provide indicators of learning outcomes. A department's publications and public statements, which may discuss and provide evidence of the quality of teaching and learning among its faculty, is another source of information.

At the institutional level, several documents address the criteria listed: the faculty handbook, the catalogue, and other publications that describe institutional policies and practices are important sources of information. So, too, is the institution's annual calendar of events and, in particular, its record of faculty attendance at relevant seminars, symposia, and workshops. In addition to these data of record, surveys and interviews of selected administrators, faculty, and students should provide insights.

The criteria and sources of information discussed provide valid evidence and are the basis for valid decisions. Those decisions can be made by an institution as part of a self-study or as an audit of its environment. Accrediting teams or other outside evaluators may also use the criteria to make judgments about the scholarship of teaching at the various levels of an institution.

Summary

Effective and scholarly teaching is deep, personal, multidimensional, and dynamic. The scholarship of teaching requires a broad array of skills and knowledge. It embraces scholarly teaching but requires more. In effect, one could say that the scholarship of teaching brings together all of the kinds of scholarship that Boyer defined.

It requires the ability to undertake and carry out the scholarship of discovery, for a teacher must be versed in the habits of thought and inquiry of the discipline and must be able to translate the principles of the discipline to learners. The teacher must be able to solve problems and to model the discovery process as well as to be able to discover new ways of helping learners gain knowledge and skills. The scholarship of discovery applied to teaching and learning is part of this benchmark.

It requires the scholarship of integration. In teaching, a world of information must be made orderly and understandable: the teacher must place in context what has been discovered in order to breathe life and meaning into courses, classes, and the discipline. This process must extend across disciplines as well, and the teacher who can put the area of specialization into a larger context helps the learner to understand both the principle at hand and the importance of integration itself.

But the investigation and synthesis that reflect both the scholarships of discovery and integration are not enough. The scholarship of teaching also involves the scholarship of application, because the theories and principles of the discipline are meaningless if taken in isolation. As the current terms *active learning, reflective practice, experiential learning,* and others suggest, it is the involvement of the learner, who applies principles and theories to consequential problems in and beyond the discipline, that brings knowledge to life. If education is to have meaning and learners are to become reflective practitioners, they must be engaged in the discipline and its application.

Boyer said, "The work of the professor becomes consequential only when it is understood by others. . . . When defined as scholarship, however, teaching both educates and entices future scholars" (1990, p. 23). The person who demonstrates the scholarship of teaching, then, embodies all the forms of scholarship and directs them toward the goal of creating future scholars and arming them with the necessary skills and habits of thought and action that maintain the ongoing cycle of learning and teaching and teaching and learning. Scholars care deeply about their disciplines and about their work. In the scholarship of teaching, the teacher cares deeply about the discipline but, equally, about the learners and their connection to both the material, the discipline, and learning. This is the investment of self that Palmer (1983) refers to when he speaks about "the kind of community that teaching and learning require" (p. 89), the joint discovery of the beauty and power of understanding and the scholarship that enables it.

References

Angelo, T. A., and Cross, K. P. *Classroom Assessment Techniques: A Handbook for College Teachers.* (2nd ed.) San Francisco: Jossey-Bass, 1993.

Boyer, E. L. *Scholarship Reconsidered: Priorities of the Professoriate.* Princeton, N.J.: Carnegie Foundation for the Advancement of Teaching, 1990.

Brinko, K. T., and Menges, R. J. (eds.). *Practically Speaking: A Sourcebook for Instructional Consultants in Higher Education.* Stillwater, Okla.: New Forums Press, 1997.

Cross, K. P., and Angelo, T. A. *Classroom Assessment Techniques: A Handbook for Faculty.* Ann Arbor, Mich.: National Center for Research to Improve Postsecondary Teaching and Learning, 1988.

Cross, K. P., and Steadman, M. H. *Classroom Research: Implementing the Scholarship of Teaching.* San Francisco: Jossey-Bass, 1996.

Davis, B. G. *Tools for Teaching.* San Francisco: Jossey-Bass, 1993.

Ebel, K. E. *The Cult of Teaching: A Guide to Mastering the Professor's Art.* San Francisco: Jossey-Bass, 1977.

Glassick, C. E., Huber, M. T., and Maeroff, G. I. *Scholarship Assessed: Evaluation of the Professoriate.* San Francisco: Jossey-Bass, 1997.

Hativa, N., and Marincovich, M. *Disciplinary Differences in Teaching and Learning: Implications for Practice.* New Directions for Teaching and Learning, no. 64. San Francisco: Jossey-Bass, 1995.

Kreber, C. "Defining and Implementing the Scholarship of Teaching: The Results of a Delphi Study." Paper presented at the annual meeting of the Canadian Society for the Study of Higher Education, Université de Sherbrooke, Sherbrooke, Quebec, June 1999.

Lowman, J. *Mastering the Techniques of Teaching.* San Francisco: Jossey-Bass, 1984.

McKeachie, W. J. *Teaching Tips.* (10th ed.) Boston: Houghton Mifflin, 1999.

Palmer, P. *To Know As We Are Known.* New York: HarperCollins, 1983.

Schuster, J. H., Wheeler, D. W., and Associates. *Enhancing Faculty Careers: Strategies for Development and Renewal.* San Francisco: Jossey-Bass, 1990.

Seldin, P. A. *The Teaching Portfolio.* Bolton, Mass.: Anker, 1993.

Shore, B. M., and others. *The Teaching Dossier.* (Rev. ed.) Montreal: Canadian Association of University Teachers, 1986.

Shulman, L. S. "Toward a Pedagogy of Substance." *AAHE Bulletin,* 1989, *41*(10), 8–13.

Smart, J. C., and Feldman, K. A. "Accentuation Effects of Dissimilar Academic Departments: An Application and Exploration of Holland's Theory." *Research in Higher Education,* 1998, *39*, 385–418.

Theall, M., and Franklin, J. "Student Ratings in the Context of Complex Evaluation Systems." In M. Theall and J. Franklin (eds.), *Student Ratings of Instruction: Issues for Improving Practice.* New Directions for Teaching and Learning, no. 43. San Francisco: Jossey-Bass, 1990.

MICHAEL THEALL *is associate professor of educational administration and director of the Center for Teaching and Learning at the University of Illinois at Springfield.*

JOHN A. CENTRA *is professor emeritus, research professor, and former chair of the Higher Education Program at Syracuse University.*

*How does the wisdom of practice influence
teaching and learning? Is the influence positive?
Could it be improved and thereby contribute
more to the scholarship of teaching?*

Learning More from
the Wisdom of Practice

Maryellen Weimer

A variety of different kinds of knowledge constitute what we know about teaching and learning, and are thereby legitimate domains of the scholarship of teaching. There is the knowledge derived from empirical work, primarily educational research, as well as the knowledge that grows out of and builds on theoretical constructs and frameworks. But the knowledge that is most widespread and most frequently influences how teachers function in the classrooms is knowledge that derives from experience—the wisdom of practice. Faculty learn how to teach by teaching. They learn important and valuable lessons; hence, what they learn may be correctly called the *wisdom* of practice. And yet, despite its pervasiveness, little has been written about the wisdom of practice and the largely intuitive and experiential understanding it brings of how students learn and how instructional policies, practices, and behaviors influence those learning outcomes.

Panelists in the Delphi study showed agreement (MDN = 6.0) and reasonable consensus (IQR = 2.0) that "Finding adequate approaches for identifying, codifying, reporting, and communicating the wisdom of practice remains a challenge" (see Exhibit 1.1, item 32).

This chapter addresses this issue and aims to explore the nature and role of experiential knowledge in the domain of teaching and learning. It outlines some problems with this knowledge base as it currently exists. Experiential knowledge influences pedagogical thought and action in some less-than-desirable ways. The chapter also proposes solutions that aim to enhance this very important kind of pedagogical knowledge. Resting on an underlying premise that all of us committed to teaching and learning must promote the scholarship of teaching, the chapter argues that a more explicit and intellectual orientation toward the wisdom of practice would accomplish this objective.

Background

The majority of college faculty are not well prepared to teach. This continues to be true despite considerable national attention directed toward the need for more and better preparation. The response has been to train graduate students for current and future instructional responsibilities. As the connotation of the word implies, that training is often a short course (an orientation, an ongoing seminar, or a one-credit class) that emphasizes the nuts and bolts of instructional practice, what a teacher must know in order to survive. Some training is better than none at all, but if we use the preparation of basic educators with its significant amount of course work and an intensively supervised and evaluated student teaching experience as the benchmark, most new Ph.D.'s still assume their first academic positions woefully unprepared to teach.

As a result, most of what is learned about teaching occurs as on-the-job training, in the isolation of the individual's classroom, alone and without supervision. It's learning that happens in the school of hard knocks, often by the seat of our pants, to mix a couple of common metaphors. It's the kind of tough learning that happens when a physics postdoc first teaches the required physics for poets course and encounters passive, unmotivated learners with little knowledge and even less interest in the world that has totally consumed the postdoc's life. It's discovering that students' reading skills aren't up to the book that's been selected or that students can't do application problems on a test even though they have been given all the necessary tools.

Most faculty adjust, adapt, and move on to become better teachers. Now, twenty years later, we veterans shudder when we recall some of the things we tried at the beginning. We have learned a lot about teaching. But our experiential understandings are intuitive; feelings in our guts dictate what we do and don't do in the classroom. Most of us struggle to articulate the rationale behind the instructional choices we've made. We can't explain it in terms of some theoretical framework, nor can we justify it in terms of experimental findings. We just know that the efficacy of what we do has proven itself in the crucible of our classrooms. Sometimes, our lengthy, successful experience with a particular approach motivates us to propose it for and to others. Having been there and done that, we endorse what we propose with the passion that derives from positive, firsthand experience.

The pervasiveness of this experientially derived wisdom of practice is reflected in the literature of the pedagogical practitioner. The pedagogical periodicals of our respective disciplines (*Journal of Chemical Education, Teaching of Sociology, Journal of Engineering Education, Journal of College Science Teaching,* to name but a few) and some more generic pedagogical periodicals (*College Teaching* and *Journal on Excellence in College Teaching,* for example) contain many articles premised on little more than the author's firsthand experience (compare also Richlin's discussion, in the following chapter, of problems common to articles rejected by the *Journal on Excellence in College Teaching*): "I tried this, and I know it works." Many of the ideas proposed are excellent and undoubtedly successful for the teachers who use them and the students who learn from them. There is no reason to discredit the good techniques of pedagogical practice. The objections about to be explored focus not on the techniques, strategies, and approaches but on the intuitive, nonreflective, and often uninformed knowledge base on which they rest.

Unfortunately, the national dialogue on teaching and learning often furthers an analysis of technique focused largely on experiential details. Discussions of teaching and learning, whether they occur between individual faculty members, in the context of faculty development workshops, or at national meetings where disciplinary colleagues address pedagogical issues, too often and too exclusively center on instructional mechanics—how you do group work, how you assess projects, how you encourage participation, how you incorporate technology, and so on. Much less often does the dialogue address the larger issues of philosophy, rationale, and intended outcomes—the *why* questions. The net result is a wisdom of practice more mechanical and superficial than it could or should be. Teaching scholars could better promote issues of teaching and learning if they handled the wisdom of practice in more reflective, complex, and substantive ways.

Problems with Our Current Wisdom of Practice

The goal of this section is to delineate five specific problems reflected in the current experiential knowledge base for teaching and learning. Interestingly, these problems exist when the domain of reference is the practice of an individual faculty member in a classroom or when that individual writes about a specific technique, and when the domain is the collective wisdom of practice for a discipline as it might be exemplified in that field's pedagogical periodical. I use examples to illustrate particular problems in both domains. Interconnections exist between and among the individual problems, and they add further to the diminution of the current wisdom of practice.

Problem One. The wisdom of practice exists independent of theoretical or conceptual frameworks. The problem here involves a lack of relevant background knowledge. The success of many techniques and approaches (as well as the failure of others) can often be explained in terms of well-known and documented theories or principles. To illustrate, the principles of constructive feedback as they have been described and tested in many contexts including education and counseling, for example, easily and obviously account for the success of techniques that propose ways of using positive feedback, ways of providing prompt feedback, and ways of involving peers in the delivery of feedback. Or consider this example: for as long as I can remember, I've heard faculty complain and bemoan the fact that the students who show up for the review session don't need to be there and the ones who could benefit don't come. Karabenick (1998) edited a difficult but absolutely first-rate anthology on what is known about help-seeking behavior generally but with specific application to educational contexts. According to the book's contributors, we should not be surprised by who shows up to review sessions, and there are ways we can recast policies and practices that might dramatically influence who comes for help.

Our concern with the details necessary for successful execution of a strategy or technique gives the impression that why something works is all a matter of management, when the real reasons for success (and failure) are more often explained by relevant theory and conceptual frameworks. Obviously, techniques work less effectively when the execution is sloppy, so implementation details do merit attention. However, we must also be concerned with the larger reasons to which we can attribute the success and failure of any given instructional strategy or approach.

Problem Two. The wisdom of practice is not well connected to empirical outcomes. Individual educational practitioners and disciplinary publications are not well informed about educational research. And blame for this ignorance goes in lots of different directions. In the direction of faculty goes blame for assumptions that trivialize the complexity of teaching and learning. The lack of emphasis on education in graduate school perpetrate longstanding assumptions as to the ascendancy of content knowledge: if you know it, you can teach it. In the direction of professional associations and other disciplinary groups goes blame for bad-mouthing and otherwise trivializing educational research. True, not all educational research is excellent, but is all work in any field equally meritorious? And is that a valid excuse for avoiding all knowledge of empirical findings?

The better disciplinary pedagogical periodicals do publish research. However, most often it is research conducted within the context of the discipline—an empirical inquiry into the effects of two different note-taking strategies on specified learning outcomes in beginning management courses, for example. Most disciplinary pedagogical research has two characteristics that compromise its credibility. First, whatever the educational phenomenon, it is studied with the research paradigms of the discipline—so that if the field is economics, the educational study uses the methodological approaches and perspectives of the field. The problem, of course, is the implicit assumption that educational phenomena behave like economic phenomena and so can be studied the same way. Second, when disciplinary studies review the relevant literature, they seldom look beyond the discipline—so a study in the journal *Teaching of Psychology* may be well referenced in terms of previous research work (most such studies are), but it cites only the work in psychology (mostly previous issues of *Teaching of Psychology*), despite the fact that what's being studied may have been investigated extensively in other disciplines or in educational research.

But blame goes to education as well. Like many disciplines, it has little commitment to or interest in the research-practice interface. Educational research is written to inform subsequent research. There is no expectation that researchers will explore or even speculate as to implications for practice. Like many disciplines, education offers little in the way of reward and recognition for the scholarship of application—that difficult work of making complex empirical methodologies and qualified conclusions understandable and applicable in nonempirical environments. That work is left to the few of us who, for mostly personal and idealistic reasons, think that if we build bridges between research and practice, the road will more directly lead to better teaching and learning. And because there is this disconnection between research and practice, researchers end up asking questions that are relevant to them. In some cases, the questions are not particularly relevant or of much interest to classroom practitioners.

But after the finger-pointing, the fact remains: pedagogical practice is generally not influenced by educational research. There are simply no professional expectations that one keep abreast of educational developments in the same way that one keeps abreast of content developments within the discipline. We must find ways to promote the expectation that whatever we may be doing in the classroom and proposing as good practice in pedagogical publications be advocated in light of relevant empirical work. Good teaching and learning outcomes are not the result of instructional magic. There are reasons why things do or don't work, and many of those hypotheses have already been verified empirically.

Problem Three. The wisdom of practice generally ignores the peculiarities of fit. For individual practitioners and in disciplinary dialogue, there is seldom any sense of why some strategies, policies, practices, ideas, techniques, and approaches work in some contexts and not in others. When the individual faculty member goes to a daylong workshop on active learning and is presented with a variety of different strategies—things to do to get students involved in class, say—how does that faculty member decide what to try tomorrow? Most often the decision is visceral and emotional: "that will never work with my students"; "you can't do that when you're in a lab"; "I'm not comfortable doing that." This quick, intuitive assessment may or may not be accurate.

Missing from the body of knowledge that comprises the wisdom of practice are explorations that aim to identify the characteristics of teachers, students, content, and context that explain why some approaches work for some people and not for others, or work sometimes but not other times, even for the same teacher. We understand the influence of these variables intuitively—we know we can ask in the literature class as we seek to begin discussion of the assigned reading, "Well, what do you think of it?" but we cannot begin a similar discussion in the chemistry class by pointing to the periodic table and asking the same question.

But bashing intuitive knowledge will not help either. Intuition is a legitimate way of knowing, but there are problems when so much of the knowledge base exists at this level. Consider an example: an individual faculty member tries a new technique that does not work. From the faculty member's perspective, it was an embarrassing disaster, which typically motivates one of three responses. First, the faculty member decides against innovation. The old ways of teaching are more dependable, and the commitment to them increases. Second, the faculty member decides against that particular new technique and moves on to try something else. Both of these responses ignore what happened and do not involve the kind of careful, in-depth analysis that would allow the faculty member to figure out what went wrong and how what was tried might be changed. The unanswered question is whether it's a case of just not doing the analysis and adaptation or whether it's a case of not knowing how to do either.

The third response does involve adaptation. Effective teachers seem to know how to adapt and change techniques before they implement them, and those changes do take into account the nature of the content, the students, the instructional setting, and the teacher's style. And good teachers know how to tinker after the fact. They fuss around with assignments, activities, approaches, and techniques so that they evolve into something that ends up working well. In this case, faculty can identify the parts of the approach they have changed, but they cannot explain why this way of doing something works better, nor can they extrapolate from the changes a larger set of principles that could be used by less-experienced and less-effective faculty to increase the likelihood of success with new approaches.

Could this unwillingness or inability to deal with notions of fit and adaptation explain why so much instructional practice remains unchanged? Consider that we have now twenty-five years of organized faculty development efforts. That movement has spawned a rich legacy that has expanded and enriched the instructional repertoire, but much of it is not appropriated by individual faculty who continue to teach as they have always taught. Why is that? Could it be that we and they do not understand the peculiarities of fit? That we and they cannot modify generic approaches so that they fit the instructor, students, content, and context in which they are being used?

What happens when individual faculty embrace and then reject the latest instructional innovations can end up being a microcosm for what happens in the larger disciplinary and even national contexts. If you regularly read the disciplinary periodicals and the more broadly based higher education publications, you see ideas come and go with the regularity of the seasons. Right now, group work is in, and lecturing is out. At the disciplinary level as well as the individual level, we approach better teaching and more learning by flitting from one novel approach to the next. The process creates the expectation that better teaching is just one new technique away. The quest is for the magic technique, not the more pedantic design and redesign of well-known approaches. Not everything being proposed now is improved and better than everything we've done in the past. Could it be that we move so quickly and easily from one trendy new approach to the next in order to avoid the more difficult and challenging work of figuring out how and why a technique fits the peculiarities of our many varied instructional situations?

Examples in the current literature illustrate the kind of concern with fit that can benefit practice enormously. Take recent attempts to differentiate between collaborative and cooperative group learning tasks. Some of this work traces the theoretical and empirical frameworks out of which these two approaches have grown. Other work specifies the kind of tasks that work best for each. Still others have speculated as to which disciplines might be better suited for one approach over the other, based on the way content is configured. And finally others have offered insight as to developmental issues, in this case involving risk and control, that might explain why some faculty gravitate to one approach over another. Individual faculty must do this for and with techniques they propose to import into their own teaching, and disciplines must explore the same issues in the larger field-specific contexts.

Problem Four. The wisdom of practice exists in an ahistorical context. Solomon was right: there is nothing new under the sun. And this does apply to instructional techniques. When you consider all the teachers in all the countries across all the centuries, it is not hard to imagine that almost everything has been tried by somebody else in some classroom in some place and at some time before. So the faculty fixation with the new technique is fed by the invigorating feelings associated with *me* doing something for the first time. The technique is new to me even though others before have spoken and written about it, sometimes extensively.

Not everything about this ahistorical orientation to new ideas and methods is negative. There is a marvelous spirit of sharing among instructional practitioners. Most good ideas came from or are built on ideas garnered from somebody else. Most faculty are not the least bit proprietary about what they do in the classroom, so ideas are passed around and on with no sense of needing to credit where they originated or who changed them in what ways. Faculty members are much more collegial about instructional ideas than about anything else in the academic domain.

A good illustration of the way ideas are shared and transformed can be found by tracing the idea first proposed by Cross and Angelo (1988) as one of the original classroom research ideas: the minute paper. Soliciting feedback from students at the end of the period in terms of what they've learned and not learned during class is a wonderful idea, as witnessed by its widespread diffusion across and around higher education classrooms. The questions asked at the end of the period now exist in too many forms to count. The technique now goes by multiple names, most bearing some relation to how the technique has been altered. There are now countless ideas as to how faculty can and do respond to feedback received on these informal papers. In short, the original idea now has a rich and wonderful history, some of which can be found in published materials, but most of which exists as a kind of oral history passed randomly between teachers. Some of the most creative and, I suspect, effective ways of using the technique I've only heard mentioned in passing, as they came up in instructional conversation.

And therein lies the problem. Most faculty feel no, indeed, have no professional obligation to record and pass along what they have learned about teaching, what is, in fact, wise about the way they practice. As a result, even the literature on technique, which is the most extensive and well-developed pedagogical periodical literature, is not as complete or rich as it might be. Additionally, much of what every teacher needs to know is not part of a common foundation of knowledge passed on to new teachers. So beginning teachers make the same mistakes and repeat the same errors their senior colleagues made—many of which could be avoided. This does not deny the fact that important parts of teaching, like any other skill, must be learned and honed in the process of doing them. You cannot learn to teach effectively if all you ever do is read books about how to teach any more than you can learn to play the piano or paint a picture by listening to lectures. But it is equally counterproductive to try to learn all you need to know about teaching as you teach. The wisdom of practice must be solidified into some dynamic yet discrete body of knowledge—a body of knowledge that acknowledges and respects its history.

Problem Five. Poor and inadequate assessment techniques and approaches characterize the way faculty evaluate the wisdom of practice. How do faculty members evaluate the success or failure of what they adopt to do in the classroom? How do disciplines judge the merits of one approach over another? Faculty members tend to rely first and foremost on their own very personal assessments of how well things worked. They usually make that assessment while ignoring their personal investment in teaching, which jeopardizes their ability to be objective. Many faculty also still ignore or give less credence to student assessments, despite the fact that students experience what faculty do firsthand. Investigator bias is relevant to and in pedagogical research, despite our long history of ignoring it.

Most faculty do not use very appropriate or rigorous assessment criteria. In too many published articles, the assessment criteria are not much above the level of "I tried it, and I liked it," or "I asked my students; they said it worked, and they liked it." Instructional techniques should not be accepted because they are popular and students like them. They should be used because they have concrete, objective, and measurable impacts on learning outcomes. And we should be using assessment criteria related to learning when we evaluate those impacts.

The classroom problems with assessment play out at different levels in professional arenas. Here, it becomes an issue of standards and the fact that despite years of teaching experience, multiple publications, and much national dialogue, we have virtually nothing in the way of professional standards for postsecondary education. Give a group of faculty members five different syllabi and ask them to rate them, and you will see major disparities between and among those assessments. So we don't know a good (as in learning-effective) set of course materials when we see them. Despite the several thousand studies on virtually all aspects of student ratings of instruction and virtually all colleges and universities using rating data in personnel and developmental arenas, we have had very little discussion (to say nothing of consensus) as to what constitutes a so-called good, acceptable, or improved set of ratings. We have only norms, means, and deviations, but no benchmarks. And so we must up the ante with respect to how we assess the wisdom of practice. That does not mean we raise the standards; it means we establish some.

Solutions

We can consider solutions in three different arenas. First, most of the problems just identified have explicit but not easy solutions. We can embed practice in relevant and explanatory theoretical and conceptual frameworks. We can make practice more aware of and better informed by empirical work. We can commit ourselves to explore the peculiarities of fit in both instructional and curricular contexts. We can learn the history of so-called new ideas and take much more seriously our responsibility to preserve and pass on knowledge about teaching and learning. And, finally, we can employ more objective and rigorous assessment criteria. We can make these individual commitments: faculty members resolve to let these be the standards that they uphold in their analysis of practice and in the pedagogical scholarship that results from their analysis. We can make these professional commitments: disciplinary organizations and national associations commit themselves to these standards in their discussions and in their publication of the wisdom of practice.

Second, we identify models that exemplify what we are proposing. On the basis of my regular and extensive review of pedagogical periodicals, let me identify several recent pieces I would pick as exemplars that depict how the wisdom of practice ought to be presented in published forms: Mourtos (1997); Sharp, Harb, and Terry (1997); and Paulson (1999). Although not many reports on the wisdom of practice have been published, I would put these in the category of *exceptional,* but these are certainly not the only three. None of the three examples breaks new ground with respect to content. All three discuss experiences with common instructional approaches and strategies. Mourtos reports on four years of experience attempting to incorporate cooperative learning approaches in engineering courses. Sharp and colleagues combine writing across the curriculum approaches with Kolb's learning styles theory to form a set of writing assignments for engineering courses. Paulson reports on efforts to incorporate active and cooperative learning in an organic chemistry class. These reports are exceptional for the following reasons: all three recognize and draw from widespread practice and research related to the approaches. In the case of Sharp and colleagues, relevant theory is also involved. All three include in-depth personal reflection and analysis. Paulson is especially insightful about the adaptation and implementation process. "It is a mistake to go from lecture to active learning overnight. It takes a fair amount of practice and experimentation to effectively employ active learning in the classroom" (p. 1139). And all three reports include a substantial amount of objective and often measurable assessment data.

Third, we must also identify models that move individual practice to larger arenas—from the classroom, to a trend within a discipline, to something even larger that we might characterize as a movement within higher education. Some disciplinary periodicals contain examples of the pedagogical work that ends up providing benchmarks for individual practice. Consider, for example, a wonderful study published in *Teaching of Psychology*. Miller and Gentile (1998) conducted a nationwide survey of introductory psychology faculty to ascertain a kind of state of the discipline with respect to the structure and content of the introductory psychology course. They looked at textbooks, assignments, and activities in terms of both faculty and student perceptions. Of special note was a part of the study that compared instructor and student perceptions of course goals. Instructors indicated that their most important instructional goal involved engaging "students in scientific inquiry about psychological processes" (p. 89). The survey found that, according to students, what the courses accomplish most successfully is a goal related to surveying the field. How valuable it is for both a discipline and individual faculty to know that state of current practice in its introductory course. Studies like this never appear in most pedagogical periodicals and are infrequent even in exemplary periodicals like *Teaching of Psychology* and *Teaching of Sociology*, for example.

Related to this third solution is our need to push current models further, explore alternative paradigms, and create new ones to disseminate the wisdom of practice. Again, let some examples illustrate how this might work. Begin with the need to push current models further: what Miller and Gentile (1998) did for introductory psychology courses, other disciplines must repeat, but then we must extrapolate to larger arenas and make statements about introductory courses in general. We must establish common practices and set exemplary ones as benchmarks.

And there are examples in the current literature that move us in that direction—consider the very comprehensive and useful compendium of current practice on cooperative learning assembled by Millis and Cottell (1998). Virtually all the most common and widespread techniques associated with this form of group work are presented here in multiple forms, and the book includes many other lesser-known iterations of cooperative learning. It's a first-rate record of cooperative learning practice, and we have no equivalent resources for most instructional practices. However, the book only records—it doesn't evaluate or extrapolate. It doesn't say that some cooperative learning approaches are better or more effective than others. It offers no principles of adaptation. It doesn't summarize the state of current practice and offer a sense of where to go next with respect to cooperative learning. That said, it is still a wonderful resource, and I laud the effort involved in assembling this comprehensive a collection.

Take a second example: one of the recent ASHE-ERIC Higher Education Reports authored by Stage, Muller, Kinzie, and Simmons (1998) does an absolutely brilliant job of making accessible to practitioners four major learning theories. It is a masterpiece of translation, summary, and integration. The learning theories are presented so that they are easily understandable; the research supporting them is summarized succinctly and discursively; and relationships between and among the theories are explored. Once again, it's a wonderful resource, but the monograph is weakest when it gets to the chapters on implications. There are two of them, a total of sixteen pages in a ninety-five-page volume. It offers few and often superficial suggestions as to how an individual faculty member should act on what is known about learning vis-à-vis these theories. Much of what exists in the pedagogical literature could never be taken to the next level, but both of these fine books could; and we are looking for ways to push current models.

We must also explore alternative models. The wisdom of practice is undoubtedly constrained and restrained as it is forced to meet the publication conventions of the discipline. In most disciplines, there is a marked correspondence between the pedagogical periodical and the premier research journal of the field. If the discipline uses abstracts to summarize research findings, abstracts will appear in the pedagogical periodical, where they function poorly to highlight anecdotal, experiential accounts. We must free the wisdom of practice and let our reports of it take forms and shapes that may better reflect the configuration of this kind of knowledge.

There are a few examples; consider an old and new one. Elbow (1980) organizes an article on the involvement of peers in instructional improvement around a series of letters he and a colleague exchanged describing reactions and analysis based on a series of reciprocal observations they completed. The letters illustrate the detailed and in-depth analysis that grounds real insight about the teaching self, and they are equally instructive when read by an outsider. Just recently, an unusual and very effective book on learning communities came to my attention. Shapiro and Levine (1999) really have created "a practical guide to winning support, organizing for change, and implementing programs." Their volume takes the how-to manual to a new and highly useful place. Their generic discussions of how to do it are illustrated with all sorts of specific examples taken from authentic experiences. The net result is a real valuing of the lessons learned from and through our experiences with learning communities. Other, more generic examples of alternative formats include the exploration, development, and use of cases as vehicles to encourage faculty reflection and analysis, and the suggestion that we develop course portfolios, much like teaching portfolios, to report the history and establish the current practice for a course taught over a period of years, either by multiple faculty or as part of a larger curricular experience such as a major, for example. And finally, we must create new models, new forms of scholarship that showcase the wisdom of practice in ways not yet conceived or explored. Certainly, technology can and should play a role in these forms of scholarship.

These solutions will help us better value and promote the wisdom of practice. They aim to address the problems identified and move this most common and pervasive form of pedagogical knowledge to arenas where its potential as scholarship will be better realized. The lessons learned in the wisdom of practice are authentic, legitimate ways of knowing. We must do what we can get to gain for them the respect and recognition they deserve.

References

Cross, K. P., and Angelo, T. A. *Classroom Assessment Techniques: A Handbook for Faculty.* Ann Arbor, Mich.: National Center for Research to Improve Postsecondary Teaching and Learning, 1988.

Elbow, P. "One-to-One Faculty Development." In J. F. Noonan (ed.), *Learning About Teaching.* New Directions for Teaching and Learning, no. 4. San Francisco: Jossey-Bass, 1980.

Karabenick, S. A. *Strategic Help Seeking: Implications for Learning and Teaching.* Mahwah, N.J.: Erlbaum, 1998.

Miller, B., and Gentile, B. F. "Introductory Course Content and Goals." *Teaching of Psychology,* 1998, 25(4), 89–96.

Millis, B. J., and Cottell, P. G. *Cooperative Learning for Higher Education Faculty.* Phoenix: ACE/Oryx Press, 1998.

Mourtos, N. J. "The Nuts and Bolts of Cooperative Learning in Engineering." *Journal of Engineering Education,* 1997, 86(1), 35–37.

Paulson, D. R. "Active Learning and Cooperative Learning in the Organic Chemistry Lecture Class." *Journal of Chemical Education,* 1999, 76, 1136–1140.

Shapiro, N. S., and Levine, J. H. *Creating Learning Communities: A Practical Guide to Winning Support, Organizing for Change, and Implementing Programs.* San Francisco: Jossey-Bass, 1999.

Sharp, J. E., Harb, J. N., and Terry, R. E. "Combining Kolb Learning Styles and Writing to Learn in Engineering Classes." *Journal of Engineering Education,* 1997, 86(2), 93–101.

Stage, F. K., Muller, P. A., Kinzie, J., and Simmons, A. *Creating Learner Centered Classrooms: What Does Learning Theory Have to Say?* ASHE-ERIC Higher Education Report, Vol. 26, no. 4. Washington, D.C.: Graduate School of Education and Human Development, George Washington University, 1998.

MARYELLEN WEIMER *edits* The Teaching Professor. *She teaches speech communication courses at the Berks Lehigh Valley College of Penn State University.*

5

This chapter distinguishes among the concepts and practices of scholarly teaching and the scholarship of teaching. It focuses on the ongoing cycle that begins with the scholarly process and can lead to improved teaching practice, scholarly publications, and presentations.

Scholarly Teaching and the Scholarship of Teaching

Laurie Richlin

Ever since the Carnegie Foundation's publication of *Scholarship Reconsidered* (Boyer, 1990), faculty, administrators, and faculty development professionals have worked to understand and implement the idea of appropriate faculty scholarship. Unfortunately, the concept of a scholarship of teaching has become mixed up with the act of teaching itself. This confusion was made greater with the publication of the follow-up volume, *Scholarship Assessed* (Glassick, Huber, and Maeroff, 1997), which attempts to describe the criteria by which Boyer's four types of scholarship should be judged. In *Scholarship Assessed*, the authors propose six standards that any work done by academics must meet in order to be considered scholarly; the work must be characterized by clear goals, adequate preparation, appropriate methods, significant results, effective presentation, and reflective critique (p. 36). Perhaps inadvertently, however, the authors treat the scholarship of teaching differently than they do the scholarships of discovery, integration, and application. For the other three scholarships, they "asked university presses, scholarly journals, and granting agencies about the criteria they ask reviewers to use in evaluating manuscripts and proposals" (p. x). For the scholarship of teaching, they did not go to the pedagogical journals in higher education but, instead, turned their attention to how the process of teaching was evaluated through review of campus teaching evaluation documents. A parallel example in one of the other scholarships—discovery, for instance—would have been to review how a biologist organized a laboratory or how a psychologist set up an experiment, rather than how the resulting scholarship would be evaluated by peers (Richlin, 1993a). Although research processes are important to review (and surely extensive review is done by both grant-making and accrediting organizations), they are not scholarship but scholarly work (that is, scholarly biology and scholarly psychology). The scholarship of biology or the scholarship of psychology can be read in each discipline's peer-reviewed journals and heard at its disciplinary conferences. It is the same with the scholarship of teaching: indicators of excellence are found in the criteria used by journals and conferences to select their articles and presentations.

Most recently, Kreber and Cranton (2000) compound, rather than simplify, the definition of the scholarship of teaching as they argue, "We contend that the scholarship of teaching includes both ongoing learning about teaching and the demonstration of teaching knowledge." Kreber and Cranton's goal is to show that faculty who commit to the scholarship of teaching engage in three different kinds of reflection on both theory-based and experience-based knowledge as it relates to questions of instructional design, pedagogy, and the broader curriculum. It remains unclear, however, to what extent the authors discuss what should more precisely be called *scholarly* teaching and to what extent they really are concerned with the *scholarship of* teaching.

The Delphi panel (see Chapter One) agreed strongly (MDN = 7.0; IQR = 1.0) with the statement that there is "lack of broadly acceptable definitions for the *scholarship of teaching, scholarly teaching, excellence in teaching, expert teacher,* and *research on teaching and learning*" (see Exhibit 1.3, item 1). This chapter addresses some of these issues and discusses them in relation to items 4, 12, and 31 of Part II of the Delphi Questionnaire. The goal is to clarify and give examples for the concepts scholarly teaching and the scholarship of teaching.

The Ongoing Cycle of Scholarly Teaching and the Scholarship of Teaching

The concept of the scholarship of teaching, as discussed by Boyer (1990) and Glassick, Huber, and Maeroff (1997), actually involves two different activities: scholarly teaching and a resulting scholarship (Richlin, 1993a, 1998). As shown in Figure 5.1, scholarly teaching and the scholarship of teaching are closely interrelated. However, they differ in both their intent and product. Because both scholarly teaching and the scholarship of teaching are vital to the life of the academy, it is important to clarify and operationalize each of them. In my view, the purpose of scholarly teaching is to impact the activity of teaching and the resulting learning, whereas the scholarship of teaching results in a formal, peer-reviewed communication in the appropriate media or venue, which then becomes part of the knowledge base of teaching and learning in higher education.

Scholarly Process. Two elements are essential to the scholarly process: (1) systematically observing the Teaching><Learning Connection™ and

Figure 5.1. The Ongoing Cycle of Scholarly Teaching and the Scholarship of Teaching

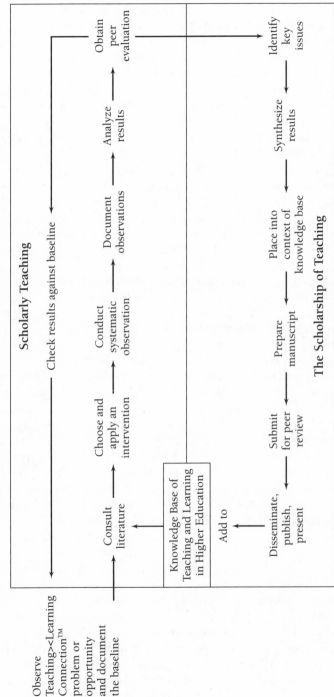

(2) putting the results of a teaching intervention into context. Scholarly teaching includes only the former; the scholarship of teaching requires both. These are the two most difficult sticking points in the scholarly process.

The scholarly process begins with an observation, which identifies a problem or situation the teacher would like to improve or an opportunity the teacher would like to seize (Richlin, 1993a, 1998). A problem could be as simple as wanting to improve mathematics test scores on a midterm or as complicated as wanting students to improve their critical thinking skills. An opportunity could present itself in the form of newly available technology or equipment.

Whatever Teaching><Learning Connection the professor wants to improve, the next and most critical step is to document a baseline of activity. For instance, what does the professor see in student behavior (poor test results, lack of class participation, and so on) that he or she wishes to change? Without this step, the professor has no way to ascertain later whether or not the change in teaching has made any difference.

The next important step is to study what others have done. This is an essential part of scholarly inquiry. Scholars in all disciplines begin with knowing the status of their field so that they can avoid duplicating ineffective practices and can build on what is already known: "As a scientific field, pedagogical scholarship must begin to 'stand on the shoulders of giants.' To accomplish this, it is essential that faculty hold themselves to the same high standards in their observations of teaching and learning as they have traditionally done in their disciplines. As the scholarship of teaching begins to develop, it seems natural that faculty will first consider methods of observation and of drawing conclusions similar to those in their disciplines. On the other hand, the natural setting—the roots—for this scholarship is in the social sciences. Unfortunately, academics in the natural sciences and humanities are not usually familiar with the basics of social science research; even social scientists who would never commit such errors when working in their fields often begin pedagogical studies without baselines or hypotheses, do not keep accurate records of interventions, and fail to report results past 'the students liked it'" (Richlin and Cox, 1990, p. 6).

Scholarly Teaching. After investigating what previously has been attempted to solve similar problems, a scholarly teacher then selects the teaching method that has the best chance of helping students achieve the learning objective. Once again, experienced teachers often do this implicitly, without making explicit why they have made their choices. To engage in the scholarly process, the teacher must justify the selection of method from what is known in the literature; it must be made explicit.

The application of the new method must be observed and recorded in a systematic way. Classroom assessment processes (Angelo and Cross, 1993) do exactly that (readers: be reminded of Paulsen's point in Chapter Two that, until very recently, the terms *classroom assessment* and *classroom research* have been used interchangeably). The professor should collect materials and reflections from observation and student work, systematically document them in a course portfolio, and follow up by reflecting on and analyzing the results (Richlin and Manning, 1995). At this point, the first of two peer evaluations should take place. This evaluation, which is an assessment of the course, focuses on course materials and student work, and may also include observation of class sessions. After the first peer review, the professor compares the results to the baseline, to see whether or not the new method resulted in an improvement in the Teaching><Learning Connection. The application of new knowledge about teaching and learning to the professor's practice is the end product of scholarly teaching.

The Scholarship of Teaching. The scholarship of teaching, in my view, builds on the end product of scholarly teaching. Having completed the process to the point of evaluating the results of the teaching intervention, the professor must decide whether or not to proceed with turning the findings into the scholarship of teaching. Clearly, this would depend on the significance of results. The professor may also consider, however, whether the extra effort to write up the material, subject it to another peer review, and disseminate the resulting manuscript would be worth the time required in terms of faculty rewards. Although some might argue that it is the responsibility of scholars to share the results of their investigations, the sad truth is that many departments and institutions do not count pedagogical scholarship as part of the faculty members' scholarly production.

The scholarship part of the process involves composing selected portions of the scholarly investigation and findings into a manuscript to be submitted to an appropriate journal or conference venue. This requires a second peer review, this time of the manuscript or proposal, by experts in both the discipline and the methods used, just as is done in disciplinary scholarship. If accepted for publication or presentation, the results and conclusions enter the knowledge base, completing the ongoing cycle.

This is not to say that all scholarly publication regarding teaching and learning in higher education must be research studies. Other types of scholarship include integration of the findings of others and inspiration in the form of reflection from experienced teachers. And this basic social science research model includes qualitative research where observation of teaching and learning behavior contributes to knowledge of the Teaching><Learning Connection.

Institutional Programs That Encourage Teaching Scholarship

Three programs provide examples of ways by which institutions are encouraging faculty members to become scholarly teachers and contribute to the scholarship of teaching.

Miami University. One of the longest-running programs, which began in 1978 with a three-year Lilly Endowment junior faculty grant, is at Miami

University (Oxford, Ohio). In 1994, it won the Hesburgh Award from TIAA-CREF as the best faculty development program in the nation. The program includes a number of faculty learning communities: one for selected junior faculty (in their second through fourth years of teaching), one for senior faculty (teaching over seven years), and the others focused on specific topics such as teaching using groups, developing teaching portfolios, or building on diversity to enhance teaching (Cox, 1995, 2001). Each learning community enables its members to participate in a two-semester series of special activities and to pursue individual projects relating to teaching. In addition, members attend national conferences where the scholarship of teaching is presented, including the Lilly Conference on College and University Teaching, held on the Miami University campus. The university also cosponsors six regional Lilly Conferences through the International Alliance of Teacher Scholars and publishes the *Journal on Excellence in College Teaching,* a peer-reviewed, multidisciplinary journal providing a forum for the scholarship of teaching.

Lilly Conference on College and University Teaching. An early outgrowth of Miami University's original grant from the Lilly Endowment is the Lilly Conference on College and University Teaching, held each November since 1980. In 1999, five hundred participants attended the conference in Ohio, representing 154 colleges and universities in the United States, Canada, and other countries; approximately 145 presenters shared their scholarship of teaching through panels, seminars, workshops, and plenary sessions. An additional one thousand faculty members participated in the regional conferences the same year.

Presentations for the conferences are selected through a peer review process, with review committees formed for each regional conference with faculty from cosponsoring institutions and members of the International Alliance of Teacher Scholars with expertise in relevant teaching-learning areas. Proposals may be interdisciplinary or specific to one or a group of disciplines. To have a proposal accepted, the faculty member must demonstrate excellence in at least one of the following categories:

Research: Reports important results from own experience or research; describes problem clearly; provides baseline data; and explains what was done and why

Integration: Integrates the research of others in a meaningful way; compares theories; critiques results; and provides context for future exploration

Innovation: Proposes innovation in theory, approach, or process of teaching; provides original, creative ideas based on research results from self or others; and outlines strategy for testing innovation's effectiveness

Inspiration: Provides inspiration for teaching excellence, combining personal values, insight, and experience to communicate enthusiasm and dedication to outstanding teaching

These criteria are listed in the call for proposals put out by the International Alliance of Teacher Scholars, Inc., every year.

Presentation proposals are reviewed with a decision tree (see Figure 5.2) that separates reports on teaching projects from philosophical or reflective presentations. For teaching projects, if the project has been completed and results are presented, the proposal is sent for peer review. If the project has not been completed or results are not available, the proposal is accepted for a poster session. Poster sessions are recommended for novice scholars of teaching to present ongoing teaching projects that have not been designed as research projects, have not been completed, or have not been connected to other knowledge in the field. In a poster session, the presenter does not have to make a formal presentation, but the printed material provided is designed and displayed in such a way that it gives readers an idea of the project that is under way and provokes discussion of the issues highlighted by the poster. Poster sessions provide an opportunity for faculty to display what they have done and to receive feedback on both their content and process. Philosophical or reflective presentation proposals from well-known exemplary teachers or scholars of teaching are sent to the committee for review, as are proposals for presentations that are inspiring or present a good argument. Proposals are rejected if they do not meet any of these criteria.

Figure 5.2. Lilly Conference Proposal Review Decision Tree

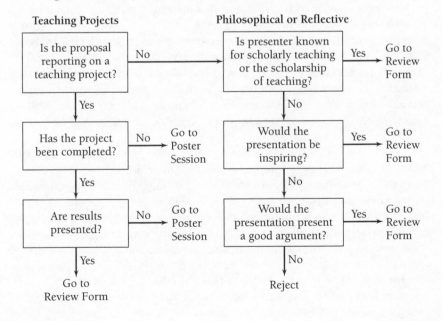

On the review form, reviewers on the committees rate each proposal unsatisfactory, acceptable, or excellent on the following aspects: importance of the topic, clarity of objectives, appropriateness of objectives, clarity of activities, appropriateness of activities, clarity of description, and appropriateness of description.

The Journal on Excellence in College Teaching. The journal began publication in 1990 and currently publishes three issues per year. It provides a written forum for discussion by faculty about all areas affecting teaching and learning, and gives faculty the opportunity to "share proven, innovative pedagogies and thoughtful, inspirational insights about teaching" (Miami University, 1999). Manuscripts must display excellence in at least one of the categories listed above for the Lilly Conferences: research, integration, innovation, or inspiration.

The editorial board selects reviewers from nominations; they represent a wide array of disciplines and institutions. They assess each manuscript on the quality of writing; organization of ideas; importance of the problem; creativity; quality or completeness of the literature it reviews; conceptual grounding; research design and method; quality and representativeness of data; suitability of data analysis; presentation of data analysis; discussion of limitations; adequacy of conclusions or implications; and relevance to the journal criteria (Miami University, 1999). The acceptance rate for manuscripts is approximately 12 percent, with the majority of submissions rejected because of the lack of research design (Richlin and Cox, 1994).

University of Georgia. The University of Georgia (UGA) also has two learning communities that focus on scholarly teaching. The Lilly Teaching Fellows Program, established in 1984, is open to ten junior faculty members (in the first through third year of teaching). Lilly teaching fellows develop instructional improvement proposals to implement during their fellows year. The Senior Teaching Fellows Program provides eight experienced faculty (who have been at UGA at least five years and have the rank of associate or full professor) an opportunity to focus on undergraduate education and share ideas with other innovative teachers outside their own discipline. The senior fellows also design and implement an instructional project to strengthen courses and teaching methods.

The Georgia Governor's Teaching Fellows Program, sponsored jointly by the Institute of Higher Education and the Office of Instructional Support and Development at UGA, was established in 1995 by the Honorable Zell Miller, governor of Georgia from 1990 to 1998, to provide Georgia's higher education faculty, both public and private, with expanded opportunities for developing important teaching skills in a scholarly way. The program creates a statewide community of scholars that engage in collegial dialogue about teaching. Many of the teaching fellows submit proposals for peer review to present their findings at the Lilly Conference held in Georgia each year.

Samford University. The newest of the three programs is the problem-based learning (PBL) initiative at Samford University (Birmingham, Ala.), part of an endowment grant from the Pew Charitable Trusts. The Samford PBL team of academic advisors, faculty leaders, and student leaders serve as advisors and supporters of the PBL project. Using disciplinary peer teams, Samford faculty members investigate PBL and other strategies in their disciplines and design units to include PBL in a particular course. Faculty collect data systematically, and each peer team reflects on the process and analyzes the results. Faculty members then change the courses based on the data collected and collect further data after making those changes. This process is a perfect example of scholarly teaching.

Each team also produces a detailed course portfolio that includes the data and reflections, all of which are reviewed externally by carefully selected scholars of teaching in higher education. The course portfolio includes the following sections: introductory information, the design of the course, problems (for PBL), assessment, a reflective statement about the course, and a free section in which the instructor and team can include supplementary information. On the basis of the reviewers' feedback, the instructor and team prepare the portfolio for publication as the scholarship of teaching.

The Doctor of Arts Degree: An Attempt to Encourage Graduate Students to Develop Teaching Scholarship. An early national attempt to encourage a scholarship of teaching was the Doctor of Arts (D.A.) degree, which was introduced in the 1960s and intended to replace the traditional Ph.D. for graduate students who were interested in becoming college professors. The purpose of the D.A., according to the Council of Graduate Schools (1970), was to "provide for the development of research skills so that the teaching scholar can maintain the quality of his own scholarship and can utilize the results of research in the classroom." The dissertation, the council said, "may take several acceptable forms . . .[including] significant research in teaching problems and the organization of new concepts of course work" (p. 15). In their survey and analysis of twenty-one D.A. programs in the United States, Koriath and Merrion (1992) found that evaluating the D.A. dissertation required "a committee, principal advisor for the paper, preparation of a prospectus, oral defense, and dissemination through University Microfilms International" (p. 77), a process typical for evaluating Ph.D. dissertations.

The success of encouraging graduate students to work in the scholarship of teaching depends on the willingness of doctorate-granting departments to award the doctorate for pedagogical dissertations and the willingness of hiring departments to hire those graduates. A survey conducted in 1990 (Richlin, 1993b) exploring the willingness of departments to grant a Ph.D. for a pedagogical dissertation and the willingness of departments to hire a candidate whose dissertation was pedagogical in nature yielded quite thought-provoking results. Approximately two-thirds of department chairs and deans at doctoral-granting institutions said they would not award the Ph.D. for dissertations on the way knowledge in their field was taught or learned. Hiring departments, however, showed considerably more interest in pedagogical dissertations, with over two-thirds willing to hire such graduates.

Where Scholarly Teaching and the Scholarship of Teaching Get Stuck

Over the past dozen years, I have reviewed a great number of submissions for scholarly teaching and the scholarship of teaching. I work as a consultant with each year's group of junior faculty at Miami University, helping them form and complete their teaching projects; as executive editor of the *Journal on Excellence in College Teaching,* reviewing all submissions to that journal; as reviewer for the national Lilly Conference, and reviewer and director for all regional Lilly Conferences; and as a reviewer for the Samford PBL portfolios.

As the meetings with the junior faculty have gone on over the years, I have felt it necessary to make more explicit up front what will be required for the project to be considered scholarly (see Exhibit 5.1 for the current guidelines). The most difficult areas are the ability to clearly define the problem, establish a baseline, research and find out what others have done, and be open to different interventions. Like their colleagues who submit manuscripts to the *Journal on Excellence in College Teaching* and proposals to the Lilly Conferences on College and University Teaching, most of the junior scholars begin with their solution (for example, "I need to use the Web in my course," or "I want to use more group work") rather than with a problem that calls for a solution. The most generous vision of this is that they are demonstrating an implicit problem-solving ability. If the intervention they want to implement is an opportunity, rather than a solution to a carefully analyzed problem, they have an additional responsibility to go back and identify the learning objectives and explore whether those will be better met through their new method. The project qualifies as scholarly only if faculty do this identification and exploration.

Exhibit 5.1. Miami University Guidelines for the Design and Description of Your Teaching Project

1. *The problem or question*

   What is the problem (or opportunity) you wish to address with your project?

   Describe what you see in your students' behavior that you wish to change, for example, aspects of content (such as test scores), process (such as ability to work in a group), or climate (such as morale). Be as specific as possible in what you have seen.

   List the learning objectives that students will be able to achieve better after you implement your project. Put them in active statements, such as, "After completing this course, you will be able to define (analyze, identify, and so on)."

2. *Context*

What have others done to address this problem? Early in the program, you may not have much of an answer here; in fact, investigating the literature may be part of your project. What topics will you investigate on databases such as ERIC?

3. *Proposed solution*

Indicate how you plan to solve the problem or answer the question. Describe what you will do to change or improve the behavior you described in 1.

Are you doing anything differently than others have attempted? Why or why not? Why do you propose that your approach will succeed better than prior attempts or will work better with your students or course?

4. *Evaluation*

How will you determine the success and effectiveness of your solution and the impact of your project? Do you plan to determine pre- and postresults? How will you know that the behavior of your students has changed or improved? Note: You may not be able to obtain your results by the end of your program year. However, you should have a plan in place to evaluate your project and report on the results. Remember, "You cannot save by analysis what you bungled by design" (Light, Singer, and Willett, 1990).

5. *Timeline*

Indicate the dates of project initiation and completion for each step of your design, implementation, and evaluation.

Conclusion

Although a decade has passed since the idea of a scholarship of teaching entered the lexicon of American higher education, the concept remains intertwined with the activities of scholarly teaching. Only by separating the different activities and focusing on the scholarly process can we give each the honor and rewards it deserves.

References

Angelo, T. A., and Cross, K. P. *Classroom Assessment Techniques: A Handbook for College Teachers.* (2nd ed.) San Francisco: Jossey-Bass, 1993.

Boyer, E. L. *Scholarship Reconsidered: Priorities of the Professoriate.* Princeton, N.J.: Carnegie Foundation for the Advancement of Teaching, 1990.

Council of Graduate Schools. *The Doctorate of Arts Degree.* Washington, D.C.: Council of Graduate Schools, 1970.

Cox, M. D. "The Development of New and Junior Faculty." In W. A. Wright and Associates (eds.), *Teaching Improvement Practices: Successful Strategies for Higher Education.* Bolton, Mass.: Anker, 1995.

Cox, M. D. "Faculty Learning Communities: Change Agents for Transforming Institutions into Learning Organizations." In D. Lieberman and C. Wehlburg (eds.), *To Improve the Academy: Resources for Student, Faculty, and Institutional Development,* no. 19. Bolton, Mass.: Anker, 2001.

Glassick, C. E., Huber, M. T., and Maeroff, G. I. *Scholarship Assessed: Evaluation of the Professoriate.* San Francisco: Jossey-Bass, 1997.

Koriath, K. L., and Merrion, M. M. "Preparing the New Professoriate: The Doctor of Arts Revisited." *Review of Higher Education,* 1992, (16)1, 63–83.

Kreber, C., and Cranton, P. A. "Exploring the Scholarship of Teaching." *Journal of Higher Education,* 2000, 71, 476–495.

Light, R. J., Singer, J. D., and Willett, J. B. *By Design: Planning Research on Higher Education.* Cambridge, Mass.: Harvard University Press, 1990.

Miami University. "Manuscript Submission Guidelines." Oxford, Ohio: Miami University, 1999.

Richlin, L. "The Ongoing Cycle of Scholarly Teaching and the Scholarship of Teaching." Closing plenary presentation at the thirteenth annual Lilly Conference on College and University Teaching, Miami University, Oxford, Ohio, Nov. 1993a.

Richlin, L. "Openness to a Broader View of Scholarship." In L. Richlin (ed.), *Preparing Faculty for New Conceptions of Scholarship.* New Directions for Teaching and Learning, no. 54. San Francisco: Jossey-Bass, 1993b.

Richlin, L. "Scholarly Teaching and the 'Scholarship of Teaching': Where Boyer Gets Muddled." Paper presented at the national conference of the Professional and Organizational Development Network, Snowbird, Utah, Oct. 1998.

Richlin, L., and Cox, M. D. "The Scholarship of Pedagogy: A Message from the Editors." *Journal on Excellence in College Teaching,* 1990, 2, 1–8.

Richlin, L., and Cox, M. D. "Enhancing Faculty Publishing Opportunities Through Understanding the Criteria and Standards for the Scholarship of Teaching." Paper presented at the Politics and Processes of Scholarly Publishing conference, University of South Florida, St. Petersburg, Mar. 12, 1994.

Richlin, L., and Manning, B. *Improving a College/University Teaching Evaluation System.* San Bernardino, Calif.: Alliance, 1995.

LAURIE RICHLIN is president of the International Alliance of Teacher Scholars, director of the Regional Lilly Conferences on College and University Teaching, and executive editor of the Journal on Excellence in College Teaching.

6

Faculty must develop their own expertise in helping students learn before they can help students develop expertise. Some faculty contribute to knowledge on teaching and learning in the discipline and beyond and become experts in the scholarship of teaching. This chapter applies three perspectives on the development of expertise to teaching and the scholarship of teaching.

Expertise and the Scholarship of Teaching

Ronald Smith

The Delphi study indicated that panelists showed a high level of agreement (MDN = 6.0–7.0) and strong consensus (IQR = 1.0–1.5) in relation to the following two issues: "The lack of broadly acceptable definitions for the *scholarship of teaching, scholarly teaching, excellence in teaching, expert teacher,* and *research on teaching and learning* is an unresolved issue" (see Exhibit 1.3, item 1) and "The links between expertise in teaching and expertise in the scholarship of teaching have not been sufficiently explored" (see Exhibit 1.3, item 30).

In this chapter I attempt to clarify the relationship among these various terms. My major purpose is to apply three perspectives on the meaning and development of expertise to teaching and to the scholarship of teaching.

Distinction Between Teaching and the Scholarship of Teaching

The term *teaching* refers to the design and implementation of activities to promote student learning. It certainly goes beyond what teachers do in the classroom. Teaching includes course design and the development of instructional materials, the out-of-class interactions between faculty members and students, as well as the formative and summative assessment of student learning.

Shulman, in *The Course Portfolio* (1998), states that "a scholarship of teaching will entail a public account of some or all of the full act of teaching—vision, design, enactment, outcomes, and analysis—in a manner susceptible to critical review by the teacher's professional peers and amenable to productive employment in future work by members of the same community" (p. 6). To the extent that *analysis* means more than the assessment of student learning outcomes and includes the analysis of the acts of teaching, it might be a form of "reflective practice" (Schön, 1983; Smith and Schwartz, 1988). Depending on how the analysis is done, it might also be classified as "classroom assessment" (Angelo and Cross, 1993) or "classroom research" (Cross and Steadman, 1996).

Glassick, Huber, and Maeroff (1997) have suggested that all forms of scholarly work, including the scholarship of teaching, should be characterized and assessed by the following six standards: clear goals, adequate preparation, appropriate methods, significant results, effective presentation, and reflective critique (p. 25). These standards, however, only imply what Shulman has made explicit: namely, if work is to be assessed as scholarly and to contribute to the scholarship of teaching, it must be made public in some relatively permanent way. I will examine in this chapter the distinction between adequate preparation and appropriate methods for teaching and for the scholarship of teaching as public work.

Scholarly Teaching

Where does scholarly teaching fit into this picture? As Laurie Richlin showed in the previous chapter, scholarly teaching goes beyond being a scholar in one's field and knowing the latest stuff. As scholarly work, it includes knowing about teaching and learning, pedagogy and andragogy, instructional design, teaching and learning styles, methods of assessment— the adequate preparation for teaching—as well as implementation, impact, and reflective critique.

What about the notion of excellence? Can one do something very well without necessarily being aware of, or having contributed to, the body of knowledge about that area? Excellence is a judgment about the quality of one's work. Thus it would seem that one could be very effective, even excellent, as a teacher in terms of promoting student learning, without being able to identify any theories of learning or teaching. In short, one can "know how" without "knowing that," what Schön (1983) would refer to as "knowing-in-action." Yet in academe, the fundamental expectation is that all faculty be scholarly in their work. Being scholarly refers both to the knowledge that faculty have and to the approaches they take—their preparation, methodology, and reflective critique. It is less clear that one is expected to contribute to scholarship in all areas of one's work—to make it public, available to be reviewed and built on. It would follow that one might be an excellent teacher without either being a scholarly teacher or making any contribution (either poor or excellent) to the scholarship of teaching.

Kreber and Cranton (2000) contend that "the scholarship of teaching includes both learning about teaching and the demonstration of teaching knowledge" (p. 476). They offer excellent ideas for how one might learn about teaching through various forms of reflection and how one may demonstrate this process and the resulting knowledge. To this end, they suggest twenty-seven examples of indicators (three in each of nine discrete areas) of learning and knowing about teaching. Examples include reading articles, keeping a journal, experimenting with alternatives, and gathering student feedback. However, it seems to me that many of their examples of indicators of the scholarship of teaching—unless faculty are required to provide evidence of one in each of the nine areas of learning that Kreber and Cranton identify—do not meet the standard of being public in a way that can be critiqued and built on. For me, many of their suggestions are excellent examples of how one might be or become more scholarly about one's teaching.

In order to contribute to the scholarship of teaching, however, the results of one's inquiries into teaching and learning must, at a minimum, be public to some audience, permanent in some way, and judged to be scholarly by some community of practice.

Perspectives on Expertise and Becoming an Expert

As several chapters in this volume make clear, most faculty members are at best gifted amateurs in teaching and as scholars of teaching. I will discuss three perspectives on the nature of expertise and becoming an expert in relation to our moving toward becoming experts in teaching and in the scholarship of teaching. As one becomes more expert in teaching, one also becomes a more scholarly teacher, as I am using the term. However, contributing to the scholarship of teaching (as well as assessing it) will require the development of different areas of expertise.

First Perspective. Kennedy (1987) presents four views of how expertise influences the actions of professionals. She defines *expertise* as technical skills, the application of principles and theories, critical analysis, or deliberative action. She acknowledges that each view has its limitations, each corrected by one of the other views. For example, expertise as discrete skills misses the wholeness of practice and the judgments required to decide which skills to use and when; real cases do not present themselves as examples of general principles. Table 6.1 suggests how Kennedy's views of expertise might be applied to teaching and to the scholarship of teaching. For example, the technical skills in teaching include preparing lessons and managing discussions, whereas the technical skills in the scholarship of teaching include developing a hypothesis and selecting an inquiry method.

We can apply the principles of good practice (Chickering and Gamson, 1987) and theories about active learning (Bonwell and Eison, 1991) to teaching. The principles of reliability and validity must also be applied to the scholarship of teaching. Schön (1983, 1987) provides reflection both in

Table 6.1. Application of Kennedy's Views of Expertise

Expertise	Teaching	Scholarship of Teaching
Technical skills: the specific tasks professionals must perform	Preparing a syllabus, delivering a lecture, constructing an exam	Designing an investigation, collecting data, analyzing data
Application of principles and theories: to specific cases, using what is known	Active learning principles, principles of good practice	Reliability, validity, generalizability
Critical analysis: a particular paradigm for examining and interpreting	Case methods, problem-based teaching, centered on students	Quantitative approaches, narrative inquiry, action research
Deliberative action: the interactive relationship between analysis and action	Reflective conversations about teaching, Schön's reflective practicum (1987)	Reflective conversations about studying teaching, Pew Scholars program

Source: Adapted from Kennedy, 1987.

and on action as an alternative theoretical framework to technical rationality for the education of professionals. Schön (1995) suggests that the new scholarships, including teaching, will require a new epistemology—a reconsideration of the traditional ideas about rigor and relevance.

Kennedy's view of expertise as critical analysis suggests that experts have professional paradigms that inform how they set and solve problems. In teaching, such a professional paradigm might be a particular approach to or philosophy of teaching, for example, problem-based teaching or student-centered teaching. In the scholarship of teaching, it might be a particular approach to inquiry into one's practice, such as action research, narrative inquiry, or controlled experiments. Some of these approaches may be familiar to you, and others may not. How to represent the scholarship of teaching is one of the unresolved issues in this area. There are ways to portray one's knowledge about teaching and learning that go beyond the usual research paper or conference presentation. The teaching portfolio, for example, was shown to be an appropriate way for documenting one's knowledge and continuing development as a teacher (Edgerton, Hutchings, and Quinlan, 1991; Kreber, 2001). Presently, however, these alternative forms of portraying or providing evidence for one's knowing about teaching are practiced by only a small percentage of our faculty. I would suggest, therefore, that the abilities needed to create these portrayals will need to be explicitly taught and developed.

In the deliberative action approach to expertise, Kennedy assumes that experience contributes to the development of expertise only if practitioners can learn from it. Practitioners must have a body of experience on which to draw and the ability to conduct mental experiments, critically evaluate the outcomes, and revise the definition of the situation. Acquiring expertise in this sense requires that one deliberate to define problems and solutions, act on these deliberations, and then evaluate one's actions in light of one's original formulations of goals and problems.

Table 6.1 shows that one distinction between teaching and the scholarship of teaching is the content of the deliberation. The focal point for deliberate action in teaching is on the teaching itself (how can I best teach this idea to this student?). To the extent that the outcomes of these deliberations are private, the learning that results will contribute only to one's own teaching expertise. However, the scholarship of teaching is necessarily public, part of some community of teaching practitioners. Thus, the focus of deliberation becomes the act of scholarship itself (how can I best study, investigate, or publicize my experiments with teaching this idea to students like this?). Schön's ideas about epistemology (1995)—what counts as knowledge and how it is acquired, the relationship between theory and practice, how knowledge informs action—are important both for teaching and for the scholarship of teaching.

Because deliberation requires experience, action, and "appreciative systems" (Schön, 1983, 1987), the expert teacher needs both experience and reference points for deciding whether his or her actions are producing the desired outcomes. Those who contribute to the scholarship of teaching, on the other hand, will need experience and appreciative systems in studying the acts of teaching, in making them public, and in subjecting them to critique.

Opportunities for developing the type of expertise represented by deliberative action are suggested by Schön's description of the reflective practicum (1987). His ideas seem to be reflected also in the Pew Scholars National Fellowship Program, a national initiative in the United States sponsored by the Carnegie Academy for the Scholarship of Teaching and Learning. As part of this program, faculty who practice the scholarship of teaching come together to create and disseminate examples of the scholarship of teaching in their respective disciplines by developing plans for studies, discussing them, implementing them, and then discussing them further in private and public forums.

From Novice to Expert

So far, we have explored the unique nature of expertise and speculated on its relationship to teaching and the scholarship of teaching; we now consider the various stages individuals may pass through on the path toward expertise.

Second Perspective. Dreyfus and Dreyfus (1986) describe the stages of movement from novice through advanced beginner, competent, and proficient to expert (Table 6.2). Their ideas have been applied in nursing (Benner, 1984) and educational consulting (Tiberius, Tipping, and Smith, 1997). In teaching, the expert seems to be able to respond effortlessly to whatever

Table 6.2. Application of Dreyfus and Dreyfus's Stages

Stage	Teaching	Scholarship of Teaching
Novice: learns context-free facts and rules for making decisions based on them	Uses rules and checklists for designing a syllabus, delivering a lecture, leading discussions, giving feedback	Uses rules and checklists for selecting topics to study, research designs, data collection methods, and analyses
Advanced beginner: learns to identify situational elements based on similarity to previous examples	Recognizes poor climate, uninspiring lecture, or confused students, then uses rules for that situation	Recognizes areas for study, methods to use, then follows rules or checklists to implement
Competent: learns to select what is important by choosing a goal and developing a plan, then follows the rules	Can choose particular goal to focus on (for example, climate, pacing, organization), then follows rules to deal with it	Chooses areas to investigate (assessment, engagement) to focus or manage the complexity, then follows rules
Proficient: intuitively organizes and understands task, then thinks analytically about what to do	Intuitively recognizes whole situation as problematic (for example, low energy level, change of pace needed), then analyzes alternatives	Intuitively recognizes area for study, appropriate designs, then analyzes alternatives
Expert: totally engaged in skillful performance, does not normally think about situation or what to do, just does it	Intuitively recognizes situations and responds automatically based on previous situations, without apparent thought	Intuitively recognizes important area or problem to investigate and the appropriate way to study or experiment

Source: Adapted from Dreyfus and Dreyfus, 1986.

happens in class; he or she has been down these roads before, and knows from similar experiences what has worked and what should be done. The novice treats each situation as new and looks for the appropriate rules to follow. The competent teacher chooses a goal or purpose to give focus to all the information available and then works deliberately to solve the problem.

The expert scholar of teaching intuitively knows what are the most important, interesting, or significant problems in the course and what type of investigation will move the inquiry forward. The novice follows a rule book for designing inquiries into his or her teaching. The competent scholar selects a goal (active involvement or deep learning) that helps focus attention on the relevant features in a complex situation and then follows rules to organize how to study it.

Expertise in teaching and in the scholarship of teaching may be specific to situations or contexts. I may be an expert in teaching introductory courses in X, but when I move to graduate courses, I may drop back a few levels and need to develop my expertise in this area. In situations that are very familiar to me, I will have learned to recognize patterns of situations and responses that work. I may have developed my skills in getting students to participate, even in large classes. I can (intuitively) recognize problem signs and have a wide range of ready strategies to invoke. But when I switch to teaching on the Web, I must find new rules to follow in order to develop my situational awareness, make choices to focus my attention on critical information, and eventually become an expert in teaching in this medium.

Most of us have a specialization within our discipline, an area that we have developed to the highest levels of expertise, and other areas in which we are only competent, not expert. The same might be said of teaching—one can be an excellent lecturer but only competent in small group tutorials. One person might be an expert in using problem-based learning or the Web, another a novice. I expect most faculty are experts in the scholarship of the discipline but are only at the novice or advanced beginner stage in their development as scholars of teaching. Will the scholarship of teaching develop like other areas of scholarly activity, with experts in methodologies (such as action learning approaches) and experts in specific areas of scholarship—in the scholarship of teaching on the Web or in using PBL?

Third Perspective. It is important to examine movement along this path from novice to expert. However, we should also compare the expert with the experienced nonexpert. Bereiter and Scardamalia (1993) suggest that not everyone becomes an expert with experience. Not all experienced teachers do an excellent job of teaching!

Most of us think of expertise as special knowledge and skill—the better students or scholars learn or know more material. But as Dreyfus and Dreyfus (1986) point out, the way we approach and solve problems changes with experience; our efficiency and effectiveness increases because we can use patterns and learned procedures or routines. Highly experienced teachers can sense when to use another example and when to move on after asking only a few questions; novice teachers are often focused on their notes.

However, even though this efficiency happens to everyone over time, for some teachers it may lead to deepening ruts. Experienced teachers can become resistant to new ways of doing things and may disengage from the course and the class, failing to accommodate their students, the subject, or the context. They do not reinvest the extra time they have gained from their experience, from having their materials and presentations organized, in teaching or in the scholarship of teaching. Sadly, they often spend this time only on research, on the scholarship of discovery in the discipline.

For Bereiter and Scardamalia (1993), the key to expert behavior is what the teacher does with the bonus of time and energy created by having developed the intuitive problem-solving skills based on pattern recognition and learned procedures. The expert invests it in "progressive problem solving"; that is, in tackling problems that increase expertise rather than in reducing problems to fit previously learned routines.

Scholars have suggested how these ideas might be applied to teaching (Smith and Tiberius, 1998–1999; Tiberius, Smith, and Waisman, 1998): some, such as classroom assessment, are usually private; others, such as pedagogical colloquia and teaching or course portfolios, are usually available to limited audiences. The focus for Bereiter and Scardamalia (1993) is on investing in one's own learning. To the extent that any of these suggestions become more public and available for critique and for building on, they will also contribute to the scholarship of teaching.

The Pew Scholars Program takes faculty who would be considered expert teachers in the "traditional sense," who have developed that "bonus of time and energy," and encourages them to become experts in the sense that Bereiter and Scardamalia (1993) suggest—to reinvest it to "design an investigative project aimed at deepening understanding and practice related to an important issue in the teaching and learning of [the teacher's] field" (Hutchings, 1999, p. 6).

Conclusions

Everyone who teaches in higher education should be, or be becoming, an expert in teaching. This chapter has suggested that this would mean knowing more about teaching itself as a field of practice with technical skills, theories, models, and so on. This movement from novice toward expert is what many mean by becoming more scholarly, knowing more about teaching, in one's teaching. However, scholarly teaching requires more than knowledge of theories and technical skills; it also requires analysis and reflective critique. This is similar to Kennedy's view of expertise as deliberate action (1987) and to Bereiter and Scardamalia's view of expertise (1993).

This is separate and distinct from being a scholar of teaching, a contributor to the scholarship of teaching, which also requires its own special knowledge and skills. As one moves from novice to expert in teaching, one naturally becomes a more scholarly teacher. One can then choose whether to contribute to the scholarship of teaching, starting on another path of development from novice to expert in that field. Not everyone who is a scholarly teacher can or will contribute to the scholarship of teaching, just as not everyone in higher education contributes to the scholarship of discovery, even though almost everyone has been well trained to do so. One of the difficulties in developing and promoting the scholarship of teaching is that most faculty members are not trained to do it.

Perhaps the essential difference between being a scholarly teacher and a scholar of teaching (at any level of development) is the degree of interest in the wider implications and impact of the results of inquiries into one's practice.

We should recognize and promote the synergistic relationship between teaching and the scholarship of teaching. Developing expertise in teaching will require the results of the scholarship of teaching; developing the scholarship of teaching will require the cooperation and collaboration of teachers. Development in both areas will depend on the recognition of the special knowledge, skills, and training needed to move from novice to expert in each area.

References

Angelo, T. A., and Cross, K. P. *Classroom Assessment Techniques: A Handbook for College Teachers.* (2nd ed.) San Francisco: Jossey-Bass, 1993.

Benner, P. E. *From Novice to Expert: Excellence and Power in Clinical Nursing Practice.* Menlo Park, Calif.: Addison-Wesley, 1984.

Bereiter, C., and Scardamalia, M. *Surpassing Ourselves: An Inquiry into the Nature and Implications of Expertise.* Chicago: Open Court, 1993.

Bonwell, C. C., and Eison, J. A. *Active Learning: Creating Excitement in the Classroom.* ASHE-ERIC Higher Education Report no. 1. Washington, D.C.: School of Education and Human Development, George Washington University, 1991.

Chickering A. W., and Gamson, Z. F. "Seven Principles of Good Practice in Undergraduate Education." *AAHE Bulletin,* 1987, *39*(7), 3–7.

Cross, K. P., and Steadman, M. H. *Classroom Research: Implementing the Scholarship of Teaching.* San Francisco: Jossey-Bass, 1996.

Dreyfus, H. L., and Dreyfus, S. E. *Mind over Machine: The Power of Human Intuition and Expertise in the Era of the Computer.* New York: Free Press, 1986.

Edgerton, R., Hutchings, P., and Quinlan, K. *The Teaching Portfolio: Capturing the Scholarship of Teaching.* Washington, D.C.: American Association for Higher Education, 1991.

Glassick, C. E., Huber, M. T., and Maeroff, G. I. *Scholarship Assessed: Evaluation of the Professoriate.* San Francisco: Jossey-Bass, 1997.

Hutchings, P. *1999 Pew Scholars Institute.* Menlo Park, Calif.: Pew Scholars Institute, 1999.

Kennedy, M. "Inexact Sciences: Professional Education and the Development of Expertise." *Review of Research in Education,* 1987, *14,* 133–167.

Kreber, C. "Designing Teaching Portfolios Based on a Formal Model of the Scholarship of Teaching." In D. Lieberman and C. Wehlburg (eds.), *To Improve the Academy: Resources for Student, Faculty, and Institutional Development,* no. 19. Bolton, Mass.: Anker, 2001.

Kreber, C., and Cranton, P. A. "Exploring the Scholarship of Teaching." *Journal of Higher Education,* 2000, *71,* 476–495.

Schön, D. A. *The Reflective Practitioner: How Professionals Think in Action.* New York: Basic Books, 1983.

Schön, D. A. *Educating the Reflective Practitioner: Toward a Design for Teaching and Learning in the Professions.* San Francisco: Jossey-Bass, 1987.

Schön, D. A. "Knowing-in-Action: The New Scholarship Requires a New Epistemology." *Change,* Nov.-Dec. 1995, pp. 27–34.

Shulman, L. S. "Course Anatomy: The Dissection and Analysis of Knowledge Through Teaching." In P. Hutchings (ed.), *The Course Portfolio: How Faculty Can Examine Their Teaching to Advance Practice and Improve Student Learning.* Washington, D.C.: American Association for Higher Education, 1998.

Smith, R. A., and Schwartz, F. "Improving Teaching by Reflecting on Practice." In J. Kurfiss, L. Hilsen, S. Kahn, M. D. Sorcinelli, and R. G. Tiberius (eds.), *To Improve the*

Academy: Resources for Student, Faculty, and Institutional Development, no. 7. Stillwater, Okla.: New Forum Press, 1988.

Smith, R. A., and Tiberius, R. G. "The Nature of Expertise: Implications for Teachers and Teaching." Teaching Excellence, 1998–1999, 10(8).

Tiberius, R. G., Smith, R. A., and Waisman, Z. "Implications of the Nature of 'Expertise' for Teaching and Faculty Development." In M. Kaplan (ed.), To Improve the Academy: Resources for Student, Faculty, and Institutional Development, no. 17. Stillwater, Okla.: New Forums Press, 1998.

Tiberius, R. G., Tipping, J., and Smith, R. A. "Developmental Stages of an Instructional Consultant: Theoretical Perspective." In K. T. Brinko and R. J. Menges (eds.), Practically Speaking: A Sourcebook for Instructional Consultants in Higher Education. Stillwater, Okla.: New Forums Press, 1997.

RONALD SMITH is director of the Centre for the Enhancement of Learning and Teaching at the City University of Hong Kong.

7

This chapter offers suggestions for how the scholarship of teaching might be incorporated into faculty development and graduate education, and introduces a model that could serve as a framework for courses on learning to teach in higher education.

The Scholarship of Teaching and Its Implementation in Faculty Development and Graduate Education

Carolin Kreber

This chapter focuses on two unresolved issues that were identified through the Delphi study described in Chapter One. Panelists demonstrated high levels of agreement (MDN = 6.0–7.0) and reasonable consensus (IQR = 2.0–2.25) on the following two statements: "The lack of formal training for faculty on teaching and learning and faculty's resistance to such learning remains an unresolved issue," (see Exhibit 1.3, item 21) and "It remains unclear how to build the scholarship of teaching into graduate education" (see Exhibit 1.3, item 28). The other chapters in the volume highlight the differences between teaching that is good, or even excellent, and teaching that is of a scholarly quality. There is agreement among contributors that the scholarship of teaching requires knowledge of the discipline as well as knowledge of how students learn, the thoughtful integration of the two resulting in pedagogical content knowledge (see Chapter Two). There is also agreement that pedagogical content knowledge itself has a role to play in the advancement of the knowledge base of postsecondary teaching and learning. The *scholarship of teaching,* as seems to be the consensus, is knowledge that can be shared with and reviewed by a community of peers, and be built on by members of this community. With this broad definition in mind, the suggestions offered in this chapter focus more on how the scholarship of teaching can be built into faculty development and graduate education, and less on how faculty's and graduate students' teaching performance could be enhanced and valued. At the same time, we should not overlook that, according to the views represented in this volume, people practicing the

NEW DIRECTIONS FOR TEACHING AND LEARNING, no. 86, Summer 2001 © Jossey-Bass, A Publishing Unit of John Wiley & Sons, Inc.

scholarship of teaching not only further the knowledge base about teaching but also enhance the quality of student learning in their own classrooms. In Chapter Eight, Cynthia Weston and Lynn McAlpine share their insights from working with faculty who made an intentional move from excellence in teaching to the scholarship of teaching.

The Problem with Present Development in Teaching

Perhaps it is an interesting paradox of the present university culture that graduate programs purport to educate future academics in the advancement and dissemination of knowledge as it relates to the discipline, whereas these programs pay little attention to the reality that the one form of knowledge dissemination their graduates will practice most frequently upon securing a faculty position is teaching the subject to other students. If we further contend, as some of us do, that knowledge is not only disseminated but, occasionally, also advanced in the classroom, the fact that future faculty's pedagogical development has received only marginal attention within the disciplines and the academy seems all the more astounding.

To date, teaching, to the extent that it is being taught in university graduate programs, tends to be treated as an add-on to the knowledge of the discipline. Most programs allow for little synthesis between discipline knowledge and pedagogy. Although graduate programs train future faculty in the advancement of content knowledge, few concern themselves with providing the kinds of experiences necessary for future faculty to develop the knowledge and skills they require to assist their own students. In short, graduate programs, with their emphasis on educating researchers, largely neglect the advancement of pedagogical content knowledge.

With this problem in mind, I offer five suggestions each for how the scholarship of teaching might be implemented in faculty development and graduate education. I discuss in greater depth one of these suggestions—to base courses on university teaching and learning on a model of the scholarship of teaching. I refer readers also to the excellent recommendations made in Chapters Four, Five, and Eight.

Graduate Education and the Scholarship of Teaching: Five Recommendations

1. *Change the doctoral program curriculum to include at least two courses on pedagogy in the discipline.* In addition to their course work on content knowledge, graduate students who plan on an academic career should have the opportunity to take courses on teaching and learning in the discipline. Perhaps such courses could be taught by a team of experienced faculty members from the discipline and a faculty development professional. Allowing graduate students to take at least one course offered by the faculty of education and have this be credited toward their program of study might be

another way of approaching this. However, the chosen course should focus on postsecondary learning and be flexible enough to allow students to explore educational issues in relation to their field of study.

2. *Allow dissertations to focus on pedagogy in the disciplines.* Research at the doctoral level should be original and advance the knowledge of the field, usually conceptualized as a set of field-specific constructs and their relationships, propositions, inquiry methods, and validation procedures. Yet a particular field of study is also characterized by certain ways of learning about this field. Were this metaknowledge about learning about the field recognized as part of the field's knowledge base, then dissertations on pedagogy would be not only tolerated but encouraged, as it is such research that would truly advance the discipline in an area that has received very little attention.

3. *Provide opportunity for graduate students to teach and receive feedback on their teaching by those who practice the scholarship of teaching.* Teaching assistantships for graduate students should be combined with a long-term mentoring program aimed at educating teaching assistants (TAs) in the scholarship of teaching. Mentors should be faculty who practice the scholarship of teaching and who have the necessary knowledge to provide constructive feedback and direct TAs to relevant literature and research. Such mentoring, to be effective, will require a considerable time commitment on the part of faculty willing to take on this role. This will be attractive to faculty only if the institution considers their role as mentors as an important part of their scholarly work and recognizes it in end-of-year peer evaluations of their performance. Furthermore, it seems reasonable to propose that the institution should offer each mentor a reduced teaching assignment.

4. *Base workshops and seminars, such as TA training programs, on educational theory and research.* Rather than base TA training sessions largely on teaching tips for the classroom, usually drawn from the experiences of successful teachers, recognize that findings from educational research are a most significant content source for such programs. Members of the academic community value scholarship, and they are much more likely to value teaching if they are shown how teaching is supported by scholarship.

5. *Identify professors who practice the scholarship of teaching, and have them act as mentors to graduate students.* In addition to the kind of mentoring discussed earlier, in which the emphasis was on teaching performance, mentors need not limit their engagement with graduate students to providing feedback on classroom teaching; they could also offer students the chance of collaborating with them on research on learning in the discipline.

Faculty Development and the Scholarship of Teaching: Five Recommendations

1. *Introduce departmentwide collaborative action research programs in which professors and faculty developers explore teaching and learning in the discipline.* Action research on teaching and learning involves an investigation

of a particular teaching-related problem with the goal of finding solutions to make teaching and learning more effective. Initially, faculty members may need the help of a faculty development specialist, who knows relevant educational literature and research methods, to get the action research project on learning in the discipline under way (Zuber-Skerrit, 1992). An action research project is complete once the results have been shared with a wider community. Faculty development specialists could provide guidance and offer coauthorship on manuscripts for academic conferences and journals (see also the following chapter by Cynthia Weston and Lynn McAlpine for an excellent discussion of such a collaborative process).

2. *Allow faculty to contract for and focus on the scholarship of teaching for a given number of years, and allow for sabbaticals to be dedicated to the scholarship of teaching.* Following the suggestions made by the Carnegie Foundation (Boyer, 1990), I would recommend allowing faculty to practice the scholarship of teaching for a specified time without being reprimanded for not contributing to discovery research in the discipline. Clearly, this would entail that universities know how to assess the scholarship of teaching just as they know how to assess the scholarship of discovery. I also see great value in granting sabbaticals for projects related to teaching. Institutions could grant sabbaticals, for example, for developing new courses or reviewing existing courses, with the goal of using existing educational research and the wisdom of practice to inform such endeavors; for empirical research or writing on teaching and learning; or for visits at other campuses with the purpose of collaborating with or being mentored by other scholars of teaching.

3. *Base workshops and seminars on educational theory and research.* The same suggestion was made for graduate education earlier. Not only do findings from educational research provide a solid foundation for faculty development initiatives, but workshops and seminars based on theory and research may also have greater credibility in the eyes of academics who value scholarship. Also, through such faculty development practices, faculty become introduced to the existing knowledge base on teaching and learning, which will assist them in making better sense of the processes they observe in their own classrooms. Furthermore, being introduced to educational theory may provide a stimulus for seeking out further material and possibly for conducting classroom research.

4. *Establish department reading circles on teaching and learning in the discipline, and encourage team teaching.* A faculty development professional who could point discipline specialists to relevant academic journals and books could initiate reading circles. As faculty discuss the literature among themselves and with a faculty developer, they might gain a greater appreciation of existing knowledge on teaching and learning and how to relate this to each professor's specific teaching context. Eventually, such endeavors could also lead to faculty contributing to this literature. Team teaching encourages dialogue among faculty on their teaching and thus is a great stimulus for reflection and improvement of practice.

5. *Base courses on postsecondary teaching and learning on a model of the scholarship of teaching.* Many universities now offer courses on teaching and learning in higher education with the goal of promoting the scholarship of teaching. A survey of such courses offered at Canadian universities (Smith, 1995) indicated that these courses tend to be similar in terms of overall goals and content areas. To date, however, the courses follow no common standard or curriculum, and the approaches they take have been more a matter of instructor preference than of an agreed-upon theoretical framework. One way that I can see of implementing the scholarship of teaching in both graduate education as well as faculty development is by offering courses on learning to teach in higher education that are based on a jointly agreed-upon model or framework of the scholarship of teaching. I will now discuss this suggestion in greater depth.

Courses on Learning to Teach in Higher Education

I have been intrigued by the possibility of arriving at a model of the scholarship of teaching that could provide guidance for the design and facilitation of courses on learning to teach in higher education. The remainder of this chapter provides an overview of a model I conceptualized together with a colleague (Kreber and Cranton, 2000) and describes a course I designed and taught on the basis of this model (Kreber, 1999). I will conclude with a brief discussion of how the proposed model compares to some of the results of the Delphi study.

A Model of the Scholarship of Teaching. Following Mezirow's transformative learning theory (1991), a notion developed in the adult learning literature and grounded both in constructivist psychology and critical social theory, my colleague and I proposed that we all construct knowledge about teaching as we engage in three kinds of reflection: on the content of the problem (what), on the process of problem solving (how), and on the premise or functional relevance of the problem itself (why). We can apply these three forms of reflection on two levels: first, to serve as a meaningful way of categorizing the various kinds of knowledge that faculty need, and, second, to explain how faculty construct knowledge in each of these identified categories.

On the first level, we (Kreber and Cranton, 1997) identify instructional, pedagogical, and curricular knowledge as three distinct knowledge domains in teaching. Through content reflection on teaching or when we ask, "What are the various components of teaching that we can directly observe?" we identify basic design components such as knowing how to assess, write, sequence, use, or construct tests. This kind of knowledge my colleague and I called "instructional." Through process reflection or when we ask, "How have we come to think that these instructional aspects are effective?" we identify knowledge about how students learn. This kind of knowledge, we contend, includes Shulman's notion of pedagogical content knowledge and, as such, encompasses both discipline-specific content knowledge as well as knowledge of how students' construction of this content knowledge can be facilitated. However, it is also more comprehensive than Shulman's pedagogical content knowledge in that it includes educational knowledge that is not specific to the discipline such as knowing about different cognitive and learning styles, about how to foster critical reflection and self-direction in learning, or about how to influence students' motivation to learn. This kind of knowledge we called "pedagogical." Through premise reflection or when we ask, "Why does it matter whether or not teaching takes place?" we identify the purposes, goals, and rationale for courses or programs. This kind of knowledge we called "curricular."

On the second level, we identify reflection on content, process, and premise as three ways in which individuals construct knowledge within each of the three knowledge domains: instructional, pedagogical, and curricular (see Exhibit 7.1). Within each of the three knowledge domains, content reflection refers to making one's present knowledge of teaching explicit; process reflection refers to testing whether one's actions have been effective; and premise reflection refers to calling into question the reasons behind one's specific practices (Kreber and Cranton, 2000).

Exhibit 7.1. A Model of the Scholarship of Teaching: Content, Process, and Premise Reflection on Instructional, Pedagogical, and Curricular Knowledge

Instructional Knowledge
(Knowledge about various components of instructional design)

Content reflection	What should I do in course design, method selection, student assessment?
Process reflection	How did I do? Were my course design, methods, assessments effective?
Premise reflection	Why does it matter that I use these designs, methods, assessments?

Pedagogical Knowledge
(Knowledge about student learning and how to facilitate it)

Content reflection	What should I do to best facilitate student learning?
Process reflection	How did I do? Am I successful in facilitating student learning?
Premise reflection	Why does it matter if I consider how students learn?

Curricular Knowledge
(Knowledge about the goals, purposes, and rationales for courses or programs)

Content reflection	What do I know about the goals and rationale for my courses or program?
Process reflection	How did I (we) arrive at the goals and rationale for courses or programs?
Premise reflection	Why do our goals and rationale matter?

Source: Adapted from Kreber and Cranton, 2000.

As I stated earlier, the model follows Mezirow's work (1991) in that it is based on the assumption that people construct and revise knowledge as they engage in content, process, and premise reflection. This is the first proposition on which the model is based. However, we learn about teaching in at least two ways. One way is to learn from our own teaching practice: we reflect on our experience-based knowledge of teaching. The second way is to learn from existing educational theory and findings from educational research: we reflect on theory- or research-based knowledge of teaching. My colleague and I (Kreber and Cranton, 2000) propose that the most meaningful approach to learning about teaching is probably some form of synthesis of both dimensions. Our second proposition is, therefore, that people learn about teaching as they reflect on both experience-based and research-based knowledge about teaching. The third proposition pertains to the process and product dimension of scholarship. My colleague and I observe that the scholarship of teaching tends to be defined more in terms of outcome measures than in terms of process measures. Outcome measures might be student ratings of instruction (in which case the scholarship of teaching is *misconstrued* as teaching excellence), or the publishing of textbooks or articles on teaching (in which case the scholarship of teaching is construed more along the lines of discovery research). Rather than looking exclusively at the demonstration of outcomes such as existing knowledge and skill, we propose that the scholarship of teaching must encompass the acquisition of both knowledge and skill, as well as their demonstration. Our third proposition, therefore, is that the scholarship of teaching comprises both learning and knowing about teaching and that both can be demonstrated.

Taking the three propositions together, we arrive at the following working definition for our model of the scholarship of teaching: people who practice the scholarship of teaching engage in three kinds of reflection—on the content of the problem, the process of problem solving, and the premise or functional relevance of the question—on both experience-based and research-based knowledge about teaching in three different knowledge domains—instructional, pedagogical, and curricular—and demonstrate their learning and knowing in each domain (Kreber and Cranton, 2000).

Does the Scholarship of Teaching Extend Beyond Pedagogical Content Knowledge? When discussing the nature of pedagogical knowledge, I stated that it encompasses more than Shulman's pedagogical content knowledge. I would like to elaborate briefly on this point, as it seems crucial when discussing courses on higher education teaching and learning that are based on the proposed model. Outcomes such as the ability to think creatively and critically, communicate and negotiate effectively, argue reasonably, work collaboratively, and learn self-directedly have long been recognized as important educational goals; at the same time, vast social, economic, and technological changes require that people learn for most of their lives. I am not sure whether educating students exclusively in the discipline, that is, in the structure, critique, and advancement of discipline-specific knowledge—as crucial and necessary as such an education is—is sufficient to adequately address the broader educational goal of fostering lifelong learning. Are there good grounds to trust that students will somehow, over the course of their university careers, acquire the skills so essential for lifelong learning, or should these skills rather be taught explicitly? To me, it makes sense to include these broader educational goals into our philosophy of university teaching, arrived at through premise reflection on curricular knowledge, and provide intentional learning opportunities for students to acquire these skills. I would think, therefore, that university teachers need, next to pedagogical content knowledge, pedagogical knowledge in a broader sense that extends to knowing how they can teach critical reflection; creative thinking; effective verbal and oral communication; and collaborative, deep-level, self-directed as well as self-regulated learning. This leads me to propose that opportunities for university teachers to learn about how to teach these skills be included as an integral part of programs intended to foster the scholarship of teaching.

An Example of a Course on Learning to Teach in Higher Education. On the basis of the model of the scholarship of teaching described above (Kreber and Cranton, 2000), I designed a course on learning to teach in higher education that was offered to graduate teaching assistants and faculty across all departments of the university (Kreber, 1999). The course involved thirty-six hours of instruction (three hours per week over twelve weeks) and was grounded on the three propositions outlined earlier. Content areas comprised various aspects of instructional, pedagogical, and curricular knowledge. The course was theory- or research-based, in that course participants read the educational literature as it related to the three knowledge domains. At the same time, I encouraged them to relate what they read to their own experiences as university teachers, thereby engaging in both experience-based as well as research-based reflection on teaching. I structured classes and assignments in such a way that participants were provided with plenty of opportunity to engage in content, process, and premise reflection within each knowledge domain.

To provide just a few examples, participants read, with respect to instructional knowledge, about basic instructional design issues, wrote and sequenced learning objectives for the courses they were teaching, read about and identified different teaching strategies, constructed tests, and so on. Participating in a debate on teaching a large group versus a small group, they discussed when certain strategies are more meaningful, and likely more effective, than others. Teaching a class and videotaping it allowed them to assess the effectiveness of the instructional strategy they experimented with in their particular teaching context. Listening to peers giving oral presentations in class on articles describing different teaching strategies and on whether or not they would use them in their own practice, participants had an opportunity to hear which strategies their colleagues found meaningful and effective for their particular teaching context and why. All together, participants engaged in content, process, and premise reflection on instructional knowledge.

With respect to pedagogical knowledge, course participants read about various aspects of learning, including work on learning styles, self-direction in learning, critical thinking, models of intellectual development of undergraduate students, and theories of motivation. Just as I had with those aspects of teaching that relate to instructional knowledge, I encouraged participants to relate what they were reading about to their own practice as teachers and identify how this information might apply to and inform their interaction with students. Course participants also read about and discussed the notion of classroom research as a way of enhancing one's knowledge about student learning. As the course was offered to TAs and faculty across all departments of the university, I must acknowledge that the notion of pedagogical content knowledge, although addressed, was not a focus in this course. Even though I continuously encouraged participants to relate the course content to their own practice (for example, the teaching of history, physics, or philosophy), the extent to which specific aspects of pedagogical content knowledge could be intentionally fostered was limited. Nevertheless, participants engaged in content, process, and premise reflection on pedagogical knowledge.

With respect to curricular knowledge, to provide one example, I asked participants to write an essay articulating their personal teaching philosophy, their beliefs about effective university teaching and learning. Specifically, they read about and later identified their own assumptions about the purposes and goals of a university education, themselves as educators, the roles of students, their preferred teaching strategies, evaluation procedures, and any constraints they might perceive as hindering them from enacting their practice in a different way. Thereby, participants engaged in content reflection (asking themselves, "What are the goals and purposes?") and process reflection ("How did they come about?"), and some also in premise reflection ("Why are the goals and purposes this way?"), on curricular knowledge.

In the future, it might be possible to develop pedagogical content knowledge by tailoring courses on learning to teach in higher education to a particular discipline.

Conclusion

This chapter addressed the question as to how the scholarship of teaching could be built into graduate education and faculty development. I made five suggestions for each and discussed one of them—to base courses on learning to teach in higher education on a theory or model of the scholarship of teaching—in greater depth. The course I described was based on a model of the scholarship of teaching that my colleague and I developed prior to the conduct of the Delphi study. One question that must be addressed, therefore, is the extent to which this model is consistent with the results of the Delphi survey, assuming that these results serve as a jointly agreed-on definition. The Delphi process identified eighteen statements that, taken together, seem to define the scholarship of teaching (see Exhibit 1.2). The panel showed a slightly lower level of agreement but equally strong consensus on three additional statements (items 4, 38, and 47). Sixteen of the twenty-one statements suggest that the scholarship of teaching is driven by a desire to understand how students learn and how to teach more effectively, requires a theoretical framework, involves reflection and the development of pedagogical content knowledge, and overlaps with other aspects of scholarship. The model introduced in this chapter appears to be consistent with these statements. Five of the twenty-one statements in Exhibit 1.2 (items 2, 20, 44, 45, and 18) make specific reference to the sharing or dissemination of the scholarship of teaching. Item 18, in particular, suggests that the scholarship of teaching must be documented and peer reviewed. Recognizing the importance of sharing and demonstration, we developed indicators (Kreber, 1999; Kreber and Cranton, 2000) for each of the nine different reflection components in the model—reflection on content, process, and premise within the domains of instructional, pedagogical, and curricular knowledge. If accepted by the larger academic community, these indicators could provide a framework for assessing the scholarship of teaching and offer an opportunity to faculty to demonstrate their learning and knowing about teaching (see also Chapter Three of this volume). The list was not meant to be complete, and we strongly encouraged the development of further indicators by faculty. Our basic argument, namely, that the scholarship of teaching can be shared and demonstrated not only through peer-reviewed publications or conference proposals but also by peer-reviewed learning processes, may stimulate some further discussions within the academy.

References

Boyer, E. L. *Scholarship Reconsidered: Priorities of the Professoriate.* Princeton, N.J.: Carnegie Foundation for the Advancement of Teaching, 1990.

Kreber, C. "A Course-Based Approach to the Development of Teaching-Scholarship: A Case Study." *Teaching in Higher Education,* 1999, *4,* 309–325.

Kreber, C. "Defining and Implementing the Scholarship of Teaching: The Results of a Delphi study." Paper presented at the annual meeting of the Canadian Society for the Study of Higher Education, Université de Sherbrooke, Sherbrooke, Quebec, June 1999.

Kreber, C., and Cranton, P. A. "Teaching as Scholarship: A Model for Instructional Development." *Issues and Inquiry in College Learning and Teaching,* 1997, *19*(2), 4–13.

Kreber, C., and Cranton, P. A. "Exploring the Scholarship of Teaching." *Journal of Higher Education,* 2000, *71,* 476–495.

Mezirow, J. *Transformative Dimensions of Adult Learning.* San Francisco: Jossey-Bass, 1991.

Shulman, L. S. "Knowledge and Teaching." *Harvard Educational Review,* 1987, *57,* 1–22.

Smith, R. A. "Preparing to Teach in Higher Education." Paper presented at the annual meeting of the Canadian Society for the Study of Higher Education, Université du Québec à Montréal, Montreal, Quebec, June 1995.

Zuber-Skerrit, O. *Professional Development in Higher Education.* London: Kogan Page, 1992.

CAROLIN KREBER *is associate professor of adult and higher education in the Department of Educational Policy Studies at the University of Alberta.*

8

This chapter presents a continuum that represents our understanding of development and growth toward the scholarship of teaching. We give examples of each of the three phases of the continuum and explore the role of faculty developers in the development of the scholarship of teaching.

Making Explicit the Development Toward the Scholarship of Teaching

Cynthia B. Weston, Lynn McAlpine

In this chapter, we address two unresolved issues from the Delphi study regarding the scholarship of teaching. First, we address the nature of the "isolation of the scholarship of teaching from the primary work of the disciplines and of departments" (Exhibit 1.3, item 15). When discussing this issue, we focus on the conceptual isolation of teaching in general from the primary work of the disciplines, because we consider that these are often distinct from each other and not integrated. We contrast this with the scholarship of teaching that we consider to be integrated with the scholarship of discovery (Boyer, 1990) rather than isolated from it. We elaborate this distinction through a continuum of growth toward the scholarship of teaching. Second, we address "whether a scholar of teaching studies teaching as a discipline in itself or whether teaching is studied through another discipline" (Exhibit 1.3, item 13). We do this by providing examples of how we have tried to break down the isolation of teaching from the work of the disciplines and by exploring the characteristics of scholars of teaching. Finally, we discuss the role of faculty developers in developing scholars of teaching. This is of particular interest to us as members of a faculty development center, the McGill Center for University Teaching and Learning (CUTL).

The Development of the Scholarship of Teaching: A Continuum of Growth

Our goal is not to define scholarship of teaching; many have done that (for example, Boyer, 1990; Edgerton, Hutchings, and Quinlan, 1991; Shulman, 1993, 1998; Menges and Weimer, 1996; Kreber, 1999). Rather, we begin by sharing our analysis and understanding of the development of the scholarship of teaching, integrating the definitions of others with our own knowledge of teaching and learning in higher education and our experience of working with professors. This framework allows us to be explicit about how we conceive of this growth and helps us to better understand our role as faculty developers.

We concur with Shulman (1993) who discusses the isolation of teaching and calls for an end to pedagogical solitude by making teaching community property and thus more highly valued. Our framework explores how the conceptual isolation of teaching from the primary work of the disciplines and of departments is reduced as one grows toward scholarship of teaching. We believe that it is possible to reduce isolation and increase integration through the knowledge that one develops and the interactions in which one engages.

We summarize the development of the scholarship of teaching in a continuum of three phases, which is based on the assumption that all professors are experts in their discipline (see Table 8.1). Phase One is an intention to grow and develop knowledge about one's own teaching. We see this as the first phase in reducing the conceptual isolation of teaching from the primary scholarly work of the disciplines and departments: professors begin to see teaching as an essential and engaging aspect of their role, rather than an interference with their research. Phase Two is characterized by a professor initiating a transition from only thinking about his or her own teaching to discussing it with colleagues in the discipline. This phase further reduces isolation of teaching from the primary work of the disciplines and moves toward integrating the two by creating communities of professors who dialogue about teaching, and develop and exchange knowledge about teaching in their discipline. Professors begin to make explicit their pedagogical content knowledge, the knowledge that integrates their knowledge of the subject matter with their knowledge of how to teach it. During Phase Two, professors tend to take increasing responsibility for enhancing the value of teaching within their departments and faculties, thus reducing the perception of professors that teaching development centers are the sole repositories of knowledge about teaching. Phase Three is a shift toward growth in scholarship of teaching. This third phase is characterized by an intention to share expertise and develop scholarly knowledge about teaching that has a significant impact on the institution and the field. In this phase, professors are actively and intentionally integrating teaching and the scholarship of discovery to become scholars of teaching.

We have listed a representative sample of processes characteristic of individuals engaged in each phase. We have tried to place the processes in each phase from less complex to more complex. Our model suggests that professors can move in two directions in the continuum: within a phase, indicating a growth in complexity; and across phases, indicating a growth toward scholarship. It is possible to move within and not move across, to

Table 8.1. Continuum of Growth Toward the Scholarship of Teaching

Phase One: Growth in own teaching	Phase Two: Dialogue with colleagues about teaching and learning	Phase Three: Growth in scholarship of teaching
Develop personal knowledge about their own teaching and their students' learning	Develop and exchange knowledge about teaching and learning in their discipline	Develop scholarly knowledge about teaching and learning that has significance and impact for the institution and the field
• Reflect on teaching • Engage in institutional teaching development activities • Engage in innovation in teaching • Intentionally evaluate own teaching to make improvements • Read about teaching and learning • Can understand and describe principles underlying teaching and learning decisions • Can demonstrate the validity of knowledge of teaching they hold, through assessment by others, including students, peers, and administrators	• Engage colleagues in the discipline in conversations that make explicit their pedagogical content knowledge • Mentor other teachers in the discipline • Provide leadership in teaching at disciplinary level (for example, organize events for department, faculty) • Provide leadership in teaching at university level (for example, work as member of teaching and learning committee, faculty developer) • Engage in disciplinary and multidisciplinary teaching associations • Grow in understanding of the complexity of teaching and learning	• Draw on literature and research on teaching to inform institution and field • Publish and make presentations about teaching (may or may not be based on research) • Obtain funding for research on teaching • Carry out research on teaching using an approach to inquiry consistent with understanding teaching and learning • Publish and make presentations about research on teaching • Mentor others in doing research on teaching • Have a comprehensive knowledge of the research and literature on teaching and learning

become increasingly excellent in teaching and yet choose not to move toward engaging others or engaging in scholarship.

Prior to engaging in activities in a subsequent phase, it is necessary to engage in a range of processes in the current phase, but not necessarily in all of the processes. For example, early on in Phase One, a professor might move into the beginning of Phase Two, dialogue with colleagues, while continuing to grow in his or her own teaching, and later move forward into processes associated with the scholarship of teaching (Phase Three). Can a professor move from Phase One to Phase Three without entering Phase Two? We think not, because it is necessary to get a sense of community beyond oneself before moving into scholarship. A faculty member who is a scholar of teaching has reached excellence and complexity in all phases.

Phase One: Growth in One's Own Teaching. We have observed that professors usually begin the continuum of growth toward the scholarship of teaching through an intention to develop their own teaching, usually through a mechanism of action, reflection, and improvement (for example, McAlpine, Weston, Beauchamp, Wiseman, and Beauchamp, 1999) that becomes increasingly more explicit or formal. As they move through this phase, professors develop an increasing sense of teaching competence. We provide two examples (with disguised identities). The first is a relatively new untenured professor in the Faculty of Engineering who is a good example of a professor who has entered Phase One. She displays the first three attributes in this phase of development: regularly attending teaching development activities, engaging in teaching innovation, and reflecting on her own teaching (as evident in her agreement to participate in a research project with us that requires explicit reflection on her own teaching). At this point, it is clear that she is interested in increasing her understanding of her own teaching although it is still too early to know whether this interest will gradually move her from focusing on her own teaching to focusing on dialogue about teaching and learning with the disciplinary community. The second example is a tenured professor from the Faculty of Science, an award-winning teacher with more than twenty years' experience. He has a remarkable interest in teaching and has grown in his own teaching such that he exhibits all attributes in the first phase. He is a good example of an excellent teacher who has focused his interest in teaching in Phase One and has chosen to spend his time on perfecting his teaching. To the best of our knowledge, he is only minimally involved in attributes related to Phase Two. Many excellent teachers never undertake the shift from Phase One to Phase Two. Perhaps not every faculty member wants to or has to become a scholar of teaching.

Phase Two: Dialogue with Colleagues About Teaching and Learning. In our experience, we have noted that, at some point, certain professors become interested in engaging in conversations and work with others who are interested in teaching. In Phase Two, professors move beyond personal reflection and engage with colleagues to co-construct a more complex understanding of pedagogical content knowledge within their discipline and more generic knowledge of teaching across disciplines. This furthers the integration of teaching into the primary work of the disciplines and of departments.

We present three case examples of Phase Two processes designed to provide the opportunity for dialogue with colleagues about teaching and learning. Table 8.2 presents a matrix for considering the examples in terms of who initiates the activity and in what contexts the activities occur. We see three initiators: individual professors, faculty developers, and university administrators. We see two contexts in which the activities tend to occur: informal groups and formal structures. Given the constraints of space, we have selected three particularly interesting cases to illustrate processes that represent Phase Two activities.

**Table 8.2. Examples of Phase Two: Initiators and Context
for Dialogue about Teaching and Learning**

	Contexts	
Initiators	*Informal groups*	*Formal structures*
Professor	Department of Physics	
Faculty developers		Faculty of Science
University administrators		Department of Family Medicine

An Informal Group Initiated by a Professor. The first example is an informal group that was initiated by a professor from the Department of Physics. We have worked with this professor previously as he has developed his own teaching. This time he called to ask whether CUTL could give a workshop to introduce physics teaching assistants (TAs) to some new aspects of the physics curriculum. We think it helps integrate teaching into the discipline if we work with individuals in departments to respond to the needs they perceive. Thus we suggested that if he and a group of professors would work together to design and implement a workshop, CUTL would be glad to help. He agreed, and although not all the professors he invited came, a consistent core attended regularly. To date, three professors and one graduate student have jointly planned and delivered two workshops for forty TAs, and another workshop is scheduled. The group intends to continue meeting and planning workshops, and to follow the same sequence with TAs next year.

How did this activity provide a Phase Two opportunity for dialogue with colleagues about teaching and learning? It brought together a group of professors interested in teaching to discuss what seemed to be endemic issues in introductory physics courses. In trying to find solutions, they talked explicitly about how to teach certain concepts in a way that students understand. In doing so, they made explicit their tacitly held pedagogical content knowledge (for example, McAlpine and Harris, 1999), because they had to explain to others the methods they felt were most effective in helping students learn.

A Formal Structure Initiated by a Faculty Developer. In this second example, the director of CUTL approached the dean of the Faculty of Science to see whether he would be interested in having a faculty developer whose time was spent solely helping his faculty undertake any initiatives they felt were appropriate. The only criterion set by CUTL was that activities for faculty professors would have to be voluntary, which is one of our basic principles of faculty development. The dean was interested, so CUTL and the Faculty of Science advertised a joint appointment, working half-time in science and half-time in CUTL. The selection committee included representatives from psychology, chemistry, physics, and higher education (the academic home of CUTL). In the process of creating a job description, the selection committee had to struggle with making explicit how the individual would model excellent science teaching.

How did this activity provide a Phase Two opportunity? This process engaged colleagues within a faculty in dialogue about teaching and learning. Through this conversation, committee members from different fields learned about each other's criteria for teaching excellence in science and were pressed to create a shared perspective. This process also helped the group to conceive that someone from inside or outside their own disciplines could have the expertise to help them grow in teaching. This interaction broadened the perspective of both the Faculty of Science and CUTL about integrating teaching into the primary work of the disciplines.

A Formal Structure Initiated by an Administrator. This third example was initiated by an administrator in the Department of Family Medicine. The administrator requested that CUTL give a teaching portfolio workshop (a teaching portfolio is required for promotion and tenure). We recognize that there are disciplinary differences in teaching and wished to encourage department members to make explicit their own criteria to guide both the development and evaluation of a teaching portfolio. Thus we suggested that instead of CUTL giving a workshop, a CUTL member join their departmental tenure and promotion committee to help them define effective teaching in their context and to design their own workshop based on the criteria they defined. The committee met three times to define criteria and subsequently designed a workshop specifically for their department members.

How did this activity provide a Phase Two opportunity? The professor who initiated the contact is well developed in her own teaching and is a scholar of teaching. In her role as an administrator, she is trying to bring dialogue about teaching and learning into the department and thereby reduce the isolation of teaching from the clinical community. The role of faculty developers in encouraging such integration is not to give them a workshop but to help them create their own. Thus in creating the document to describe the teaching portfolio expectations, committee members were forced to be explicit about their assumptions and expectations regarding teaching excellence in relation to their department and their field. This is a particular challenge in an area in which most faculty members define themselves by their clinical practice. The creation of a teaching portfolio requires that faculty members recognize that teaching is an important part of the role of a faculty member and helps them to recognize that much of what they do in clinical practice is teaching, thus merging their conceptions of practice and teaching. We hope that they will see their teaching in a different way.

Phase Three: Growth in Scholarship of Teaching. After engaging in a number of Phase Two activities, some professors begin to see that the inquiry ethic that drives their scholarship of discovery can also drive inquiry into teaching. They exhibit increasing interest in sharing their knowledge and expertise about teaching and learning, a critical attribute in developing as a scholar of teaching. Well-developed scholars of teaching have grown in their own teaching and achieved a certain level of competence, have engaged with others in enhancing the value of teaching in the institution and discipline, and contribute to the growth and dissemination of knowledge related to teaching in the discipline or in general.

An example of a scholar of teaching is a tenured professor in the Faculty of Medicine. She is an award-winning teacher with more than twenty years of teaching experience. She demonstrates all the attributes in Phases One and Two. We would call her a mature scholar of teaching: she exhibits most attributes in Phase Three. Not only does she publish about teaching, but she carries out research on teaching, mentors others in carrying out research on teaching, and exhibits initiative and leadership. We suspect that maturity as a scholar of teaching is more likely to occur later in a career, when teaching and research are well developed.

There has been some discussion as to whether a scholar of teaching studies teaching as a discipline in itself, such as through higher education, or whether teaching can be studied through another discipline. Our position is that a scholar of teaching can study teaching through any discipline. In fact, our model of a continuum of growth toward the scholarship of teaching is based on the assumption that scholars of teaching can emerge from any and all disciplines.

Role of Faculty Developers in Developing Scholarship of Teaching. Although professors may move through the continuum of development on their own, faculty developers can and often do help professors to move through the phases. In Phase One, professors themselves are usually the initiators for their own growth in teaching. Faculty developers often provide a venue for people to learn about their own teaching through formal activities such as workshops and consultations and informal activities such as private conversations.

In Phase Two, faculty developers usually respond to professors' requests by encouraging consideration of activities that will create dialogue with colleagues within the discipline. In the physics and family medicine examples we gave earlier, the faculty developers for each had an essential role in helping the professors conceptualize the activity in a new way. The professors then initiated the process within the unit, and the faculty developers subsequently helped guide meetings, prepare written documents to synthesize discussion within a teaching and learning framework relevant to the project, and search out and distribute relevant literature. However, faculty developers occasionally initiate Phase Two processes at faculty or university levels when we can see potential or opportunities for increasing the community of scholarship around teaching. This was the case with the Faculty of Science example we gave earlier.

In Phase Three, faculty developers often work collegially with professors on a cooperative project or research related to teaching and learning.

For instance, we often ask professors to be participants in our research on teaching and learning in higher education, thus making them more aware of the nature of research in this area. As faculty developers, we sometimes analyze and write with professors about teaching experiences. We have also worked with professors to help them design and carry out research projects in areas of interest to them.

We believe that faculty developers can help to accelerate the process of moving through the three phases of growth toward the scholarship of teaching. For example, the Teaching Scholars program in the Faculty of Medicine is accelerating growth toward scholarship of teaching within that discipline. This program requires participating physicians to take two courses related to teaching in higher education, to carry out an independent study related to improving teaching in the Faculty of Medicine, and to attend a monthly seminar to discuss their projects and experiences. The progress of one assistant professor who is primarily engaged in clinical practice exemplifies this process. He chose to join the Teaching Scholars program one year ago and began to take courses that would help him develop his knowledge about teaching. As a result, he has begun to grow in his own teaching, already exhibiting many attributes in Phase One. The program also engages him in Phase Two activities: talking about teaching with other teaching scholars at monthly meetings. As well, he has engaged in Phase Three activities, carrying out a research study about the value of a particular teaching strategy in his field, a study he presented at a faculty development workshop. We find this program an interesting example of how faculty developers can accelerate the process of growth. For instance, although teaching scholars are new to thinking about teaching, they quickly are required to participate in activities typical of those who are moving toward the scholarship of teaching. However, because the structure of the program requires them to engage in processes at each phase, we note that they do not have the opportunity to exhibit the initiative and leadership we think may be necessary for fully developing into scholars of teaching. Thus although we think that potential for maturing into a scholar of teaching can be accelerated with this kind of program, because it is new, we do not yet know about the long-term outcomes.

Conclusion

In this chapter, we have addressed two unresolved issues from the Delphi study regarding the scholarship of teaching: the nature of the isolation of the scholarship of teaching from the primary work of the disciplines and of departments, and whether a scholar of teaching studies teaching as a discipline in itself or whether teaching is studied through another discipline. We have discussed isolation of teaching in general from the primary work of the disciplines but have considered the scholarship of teaching as integration rather than isolation. We propose a continuum of growth toward the scholarship of teaching that highlights the possibility of growth or development within and across three phases, a continuum that makes clear the role of intentionality within each phase in increasing one's knowledge both about teaching and learning and about leadership in the valuing of teaching. This view of the growth of the scholarship of teaching is based on the assumption that scholars of teaching can and will emerge from any and all disciplines. We were interested in how the continuum would help us understand our role as faculty developers. We conclude that if our goal is to encourage the scholarship of teaching, then we must move beyond helping individual professors to grow in their own teaching and facilitating dialogue with colleagues about teaching and learning; we must do more to support professors' transition into Phase Three, growth as scholars.

References

Boyer, E. L. *Scholarship Reconsidered: Priorities of the Professoriate.* Princeton, N.J.: Carnegie Foundation for the Advancement of Teaching, 1990.

Edgerton, R., Hutchings, P., and Quinlan, K. *The Teaching Portfolio: Capturing the Scholarship in Teaching.* Washington, D.C.: American Association for Higher Education, 1991.

Kreber, C. "Defining and Implementing the Scholarship of Teaching: The Results of a Delphi Study." Paper presented at the annual meeting of the Canadian Society for the Study of Higher Education, Université de Sherbrooke, Sherbrooke, Quebec, June 1999.

McAlpine, L., and Harris, R. "Lessons Learned: Faculty Developer and Engineer Working as Faculty Development Colleagues." *International Journal for Academic Development,* 1999, 4(1), 11–17.

McAlpine, L., Weston, C. B., Beauchamp, J., Wiseman, C., and Beauchamp, C. "Building a Metacognitive Model of Reflection." *Higher Education,* 1999, 37, 105–131.

Menges, R. J., and Weimer, M. *Teaching on Solid Ground: Using Scholarship to Improve Practice.* San Francisco: Jossey-Bass, 1996.

Shulman, L. S. "Teaching as Community Property: Putting an End to Pedagogical Solitude." *Change,* Nov.-Dec. 1993, pp. 6–7.

Shulman, L. S. "Course Anatomy: The Dissection and Analysis of Knowledge Through Teaching." In P. Hutchings (ed.), *The Course Portfolio: How Faculty Can Examine Their Teaching to Advance Practice and Improve Student Learning.* Washington, D.C.: American Association for Higher Education, 1998.

CYNTHIA B. WESTON *and* LYNN MCALPINE *are members of the Center for University Teaching and Learning, of which McAlpine is director, and associate professors in the Department of Educational and Counselling Psychology at McGill University in Montreal.*

9

Previous chapters provided insight into what the
scholarship of teaching is and how it might be assessed
and recognized; however, the question of how universities
should respond to teaching excellence appears unresolved.
This chapter revisits what we have learned from this
volume and speculates on where this learning might lead.

Observations, Reflections, and Speculations: What We Have Learned About the Scholarship of Teaching and Where It Might Lead

Carolin Kreber

In this volume, contributors discussed the scholarship of teaching, and some took on the difficult project of differentiating it from scholarly teaching, excellent teaching, and expertise in teaching (see in particular Chapters Five, Six, and Eight). Concentrating on the idea of the scholarship of teaching, Michael Theall and John Centra, in Chapter Three, offer numerous valuable suggestions for how this form of scholarship can be assessed and recognized. In doing so, they addressed one of the most significant issues surrounding the scholarship of teaching that Delphi panelists had identified as unresolved: "The assessment, recognition, and reward of the scholarship of teaching remains a primary challenge" (Exhibit 1.3, item 2, MDN = 7.0; IQR = 1.0). An item that did not appear in Exhibit 1.3 but that was identified and listed in the Delphi survey was "Whether teaching, in order to be valued in the academy, has to be scholarly and whether excellent teaching is not valuable in itself remain unresolved issues" (Part II, item 24). On the whole, panelists neither agreed particularly highly with this statement (MDN = 4.0) nor demonstrated strong group consensus (IQR = 3.0). It is not surprising, therefore, that the discussions in the previous chapters did not address this question explicitly. My purpose in this chapter is to consider this issue by revisiting the views presented in this volume.

Recognizing Teaching Excellence Versus Recognizing the Scholarship of Teaching

What does *valued* mean in the context of item 24 of Part II? Most campuses in North America now have teaching awards to recognize excellence in teaching at the departmental, faculty, or institutional level. Perhaps more importantly, many regional, provincial, and national awards exist, such as the prestigious award administered by the Ontario Confederation of University Faculty Associations or the nationwide 3M Teaching Award, institutionalized and administered by the Society for Teaching and Learning in Higher Education (STLHE), to name just two examples from Canada. Notwithstanding the praise, recognition, and reputation as a good teacher that come along with receiving a teaching award, the monetary value associated with these awards is usually smaller than awards attainable in the research arena. These things considered, the question remains, "Is excellent teaching valued?" The simple answer might be "Yes, it is valued to the extent that the award recipient values having a reputation as a good teacher, values being recognized as such, and does not overly value monetary compensation for such excellence."

Most often, when faculty speak of something being valued or not valued in academe, what they have in mind is whether it is given any weight in decisions regarding merit, tenure, and promotion—whether it is valued by the institution. Interestingly enough, a few faculty members at research-intensive universities have been promoted to the rank of full professor on the basis of their teaching excellence. This is indeed surprising, considering the well-reported bias toward research productivity particularly in decisions regarding promotion to a higher professorial rank. The question that such unusual cases raise is whether every faculty member should be expected to be a scholar—whether every faculty member should be expected to contribute to scholarship.

As for faculty's teaching role, contributors to this volume made several points. First, authors suggested that faculty should be scholarly about their teaching just as they are scholarly about their research. Second, the point was made that not every faculty member may choose to contribute to the scholarship of teaching. Not limiting the discussion to teaching as such, Ronald Smith in Chapter Six broaches the question whether being scholarly about one's work is enough or whether faculty should be expected to contribute to scholarship in some area (for example, in the teaching or the content of the discipline). Now that we have a fairly good understanding of what the scholarship of teaching is and have made suggestions for how to address most of the issues identified in the Delphi study, we face yet another problem: What are we now prepared to say to the disappointed faculty member who confides in us her perception that it is unfair that the institution has not yet granted her the well-deserved recognition as a scholar of teaching? What if, after some probing, we learn that this colleague's research or publication record seems rather weak when compared to those of her peers, yet she conveys to us clearly and convincingly that she cares about teaching and student learning much more than they do? What if this colleague has very positive peer reviews on classroom teaching, excellent student ratings of instruction, plenty of anecdotal evidence of teaching prowess, and records of participation at meetings such as STLHE , the Professional and Organizational Development Network in Higher Education (POD), or the International Society for Exploring Teaching Alternatives (ISETA), but it turns out that she has little explicit knowledge about teaching, and, apart from having shared teaching strategies that worked, she has not contributed to the knowledge base of teaching and learning? In short, what to do about the excellent teacher who does not contribute to scholarship? To what extent is or should this excellence be valued?

After pondering this question for some time, I realize that an appropriate answer has been given in this volume after all. Michael Paulsen, in Chapter Two, provides a succinct argument for how and why the scholarship of teaching is closely linked to the notion of Shulman's pedagogical content knowledge. The most direct impact on the development of pedagogical content knowledge is seen in the conduct of classroom research into teaching and learning in the discipline, which itself must be informed by, and may advance, both educational research and knowledge and discipline-based research and knowledge. Maryellen Weimer, in Chapter Four, argues for the nurturing of a wisdom of practice, one that is not limited to knowing "this is what worked for me" but one that is informed by, and further builds on, what is presently known about teaching and learning, so as to answer the question of why it worked in this context. Laurie Richlin, in Chapter Five, suggests that faculty need assistance in becoming more scholarly about their teaching and in engaging in the scholarship of teaching, and she discusses various initiatives presently in place that demonstrate how this can be achieved. Ronald Smith, in Chapter Six, distinguishes excellence from scholarship, as do Cynthia Weston and Lynn McAlpine in Chapter Eight. There seems to be consensus among contributors to this volume that faculty should be expected to be scholarly in their work including teaching and that although not every faculty member should be expected to practice the scholarship of teaching, every faculty member should be a scholar in or of some area. The appropriate response to the disappointed faculty member mentioned earlier might be to convey at least five interrelated points:

1. Excellence in teaching is valuable in its own right and should be rewarded, but the rewards for it should be different from the rewards for the scholarship of teaching because teaching excellence and the scholarship of teaching are not the same.
2. The concept of the scholarship of teaching, versus excellence in teaching, has been described and defined in the literature (for example, this volume).

3. Professional advancement at a university is based on scholarship, be this in the area of teaching the discipline, in the content of the discipline itself, in the area of synthesis and integration of knowledge, or in the area of application of knowledge to real-world problems (to use Boyer's four-faceted classification system).

4. Those who would like to make teaching the focus of their scholarship but are uncertain about what this entails may wish to consult the relevant literature for suggestions for mentoring in the scholarship of teaching and seek other assistance such as consultation with peers and faculty developers.

5. Both scholarly teaching and practicing the scholarship of teaching involve being cognizant of the existing research-based or theory-based knowledge about teaching and using this knowledge to explain practice, as well as sharing one's insights in the form of the wisdom of practice in a way that can be peer reviewed.

Clearly, this is a touchy issue and considering the process of how to convey these points to faculty will be just as important as considering the points themselves. With all the talk about what does and what does not constitute scholarship in academic work, we should not forget that we are making value judgments about the performance of individuals, colleagues, whose academic self-concept may very well be weak already (for example, faculty hired in an earlier period under one set of expectations are now compared to colleagues hired under different expectations, or junior faculty with little scholarly experience dread the call from the department chair saying that it's time to apply for tenure). It strikes me as an important move on the part of faculty developers, department chairs, and anyone who practices the scholarship of teaching and wishes to act as a peer consultant or mentor to make deliberate efforts to enhance faculty's self-efficacy in the scholarship of teaching. This involves showing them that they have the ability to practice this kind of work and to do it well. This will include talking about it, demonstrating the process, pointing to relevant resources, and so forth, processes well documented in the previous chapter by Cynthia Weston and Lynn McAlpine.

What Will Follow from the Lessons Learned?

In Chapter One, I raised the question whether what we need is really yet another contribution to the literature on the scholarship of teaching, a literature that has been steadily expanding ever since Boyer first popularized the notion in the early 1990s. In responding to this question, my goal was to make a convincing case for the unique nature and purpose of the present volume, which seeks to provide clarity and definition in a field largely characterized by confusion and elusiveness. To what extent has this goal been achieved? To what extent can the lessons that contributors and readers have learned now be shared with the wider academic community? To what extent is it reasonable to assume that what has been suggested here will eventually translate into policy reform regarding graduate education, faculty development, and faculty evaluation? Some speculations follow.

To what extent has this volume achieved its goal? Have we been able to define the scholarship of teaching? I would think so. Michael Paulsen, Maryellen Weimer, and Laurie Richlin do a superb job in articulating the meaning of the concept. As a result of the important work done by Michael Theall and John Centra, we now have much clearer suggestions on how to assess, recognize, and award the scholarship of teaching. Ronald Smith, Cynthia Weston, and Lynn McAlpine make excellent recommendations for how faculty can be helped in growing toward and within the scholarship of teaching. Yes, I think we were able to put clearer parameters on the concept.

To what extent can the lessons that contributors and readers have learned now be shared with the wider academic community? It seems to me that if the chapters in this volume generate further and perhaps better-informed discussion about the meaning of the scholarship of teaching and how it is linked to other forms of scholarship both at our campuses and at meetings of professional associations such as POD or STLHE, an important gain has been made. Initiatives in this direction have been taken through symposia at the annual meeting of the American Educational Research Association as well as the Canadian Society for the Study of Higher Education (Kreber and Associates, 2000a, 2000b), but the problem with these societies is that the audience is limited to education scholars, however. If, in addition, individuals in influential positions, such as academic vice presidents, deans, and department chairs, were intrigued and convinced by the definitions and concepts advanced here and, as a result, drew these chapters to the attention of their faculty, it could stimulate significant discussions at the department, faculty, and university level.

To what extent is it reasonable to assume that what these authors have suggested will eventually translate into policy reform regarding graduate education, faculty development, and faculty evaluation? This will depend not least on whether the communication of ideas will unfold as envisioned above. Also, this decade will witness a huge transformation of the professoriate with faculty hired in the 1960s retiring, thereby opening up positions for recent graduates. These recent Ph.D.'s may or may not have been introduced in their graduate programs to the pedagogical aspects of their role as faculty members; however, neither will they yet have accepted a reward system that values the scholarship of discovery over the scholarship of teaching. It may be with the future generation of faculty that the ideas articulated in this volume have the greatest chance to be heard. As a faculty member presently working with these future colleagues, I see myself operating within an environment that has tremendous appeal and enormous potential for change.

References

Boyer, E. L. *Scholarship Reconsidered: Priorities of the Professoriate*. Princeton, N.J.: Carnegie Foundation for the Advancement of Teaching, 1990.

Kreber, C., and Associates. "Defining and Implementing the Scholarship of Teaching." Symposium at the annual meeting of the American Educational Research Association (Division J), New Orleans, Apr. 2000a.

Kreber, C., and Associates. "Perspectives on the Scholarship of Teaching." Symposium with the Canadian Society for the Study of Higher Education, Congress of the Social Sciences and Humanities, University of Alberta, May 2000b.

CAROLIN KREBER *is associate professor of adult and higher education in the Department of Educational Policy Studies at the University of Alberta.*

Index

Active learning, 41
Adam, B. E., 19, 26
Adaptation issues, 50–51
Advanced beginner, 74*t*
American Association for Higher Education, 2
American Educational Research Association, 103
Angelo, T. A., 21, 22, 27, 32, 51, 60, 70
ASHE-ERIC Higher Education Reports (Stage, Muller, Kinzie, and Simmons 1998), 55
Assessment. *See* Scholarship of teaching assessment

Benner, P. E., 73
Bereiter, C., 75, 76
Bonwell, C. C., 71
Boyer, E. L., 1, 19, 20, 21, 26, 31, 32, 34, 42, 58, 82, 89, 102
Brinko, K. T., 34
Busby, D. M., 2

Cambridge, B., 2
Canadian Association of University Teachers, 32
Canadian Society for the Study of Higher Education, 103
Carnegie Academy for the Scholarship of Teaching and Learning, 21, 73
Carnegie Foundation for the Advancement of Teaching, 2, 57, 82
Center for Teaching and Learning (University of Illinois), 2
Centra, J. A., 2, 5, 31, 43, 99, 103
Centre for the Enhancement of Learning and Teaching (City University of Hong Kong), 2
Chickering, A. W., 71
City University of Hong Kong, 2
Classroom assessment, 21, 22, 60
Classroom assessment techniques (CATs), 21, 27–28. *See also* Classroom research
Classroom Research: Implementing the Scholarship of Teaching (Cross and Steadman), 22
Classroom research: comparing classroom assessment and, 21, 22; contribution to pedagogical content knowledge by, 27–28; Delphi study on scholarship of teaching and, 25–28; described, 60–61; pedagogical literature on, 48; relationship between scholarship of teaching and, 21–23; tracking paths of scholarship of teaching relations with, 23–25, 24*f*
Clayton, M. J., 2
Competent stage, 74*t*
Consensus, 4
Content knowledge, 20
Cooperative learning models, 54–55
Cottell, P. G., 54
Council of Graduate Schools, 65
Course Portfolio (Shulman), 69
Cox, M. D., 60, 62, 64
Cranton, P. A., 2, 19, 20, 21, 58, 70, 71, 83, 84, 85, 86, 88
Cross, K. P., 19, 21, 22, 23, 27, 32, 34, 51, 60, 70
Curricular knowledge, 83–84*e*, 87
Curriculum: on learning to teach, 83–87; pedagogical content knowledge, 80–81; postsecondary teaching/learning, 83

Davis, B. G., 32
Deliberation action, 72–73, 76
Delphi study (1998–1999): goals of, 1–2; model of scholarship of teaching developed using, 83–88, 84*e*; phases of, 3–4; revelations of, 99, 100; scholarship of teaching components identified in, 15–16, 58; scholarship of teaching questionnaire of, 6–15; unresolved issues identified in, 16–17, 100–101
Delphi survey method: overview of, 2–3; scholarship of teaching questionnaire using, 6–15; scholarships of teaching/research studied using, 25–28
Department level: learning outcomes/relevant teaching at, 39; pedagogical knowledge/innovation at, 40; public account of teaching at, 38; reading circles at, 82; sources of information at, 40–41
Diamond, R. M., 2, 19, 26

Back Issue/Subscription Order Form

Copy or detach and send to:
Jossey-Bass Inc., 350 Sansome Street, San Francisco CA 94104-1342

Call or fax toll free!
Phone 888-378-2537 6AM-5PM PST; Fax 800-605-2665

Back issues: Please send me the following issues at $27 each
(Important: please include series initials and issue number, such as TL90)

1. TL _____

_____

_____

$ _____   Total for single issues

$ _____   Shipping charges (for single issues *only;* subscriptions are exempt
from shipping charges): Up to $30, add $5^{50} • $30^{01}–$50, add $6^{50}
$50^{01}–$75, add $8 • $75^{01}–$100, add $10 • $100^{01}–$150, add $12
Over $150, call for shipping charge

Subscriptions   Please ❏ start   ❏ renew my subscription to *New Directions for
Teaching and Learning* for the year _____ at the following rate:

U.S.:   ❏ Individual $59   ❏ Institutional $114
Canada/Mexico: ❏ Individual $59   ❏ Institutional $154
All Others: ❏ Individual $83   ❏ Institutional $188

$ _____   Total single issues and subscriptions (Add appropriate sales tax
for your state for single issue orders. No sales tax for U.S. subscriptions.
Canadian residents, add GST for subscriptions and single issues.)

❏ Payment enclosed (U.S. check or money order only)
❏ VISA, MC, AmEx, Discover Card #_____ Exp. date_____

Signature _____ Day phone _____
❏ Bill me (U.S. institutional orders only. Purchase order required)

Purchase order #_____
Federal Tax ID 135593032   GST 89102-8052

Name _____

Address _____

_____

Phone_____ E-mail _____

For more information about Jossey-Bass, visit our Web site at:
www.josseybass.com   **PRIORITY CODE = ND1**

OTHER TITLES AVAILABLE IN THE
NEW DIRECTIONS FOR TEACHING AND LEARNING SERIES
Marilla D. Svinicki, Editor-in-Chief
R. Eugene Rice, Consulting Editor